Athens

D1363671

Berlitz Publishing Company, Inc.
Princeton   Mexico City   London   Eschborn   Singapore

Berlitz Trademark Reg. U.S. Patent Office and other countries
Marca Registrada

Text:	Lindsay Bennett
Editor:	Media Content Marketing, Inc.
Photography:	Pete Bennett
Cover Photo:	Pete Bennett
Layout:	Media Content Marketing, Inc.
Cartography:	Ortelius Design

Although the publisher tries to insure the accuracy of all the information in this book, changes are inevitable and errors may result. The publisher cannot be responsible for any resulting loss, inconvenience, or injury. If you find an error in this guide, please let the editors know by writing to Berlitz Publishing Company, 400 Alexander Park, Princeton, NJ 08540-6306.

ISBN 2-8315-7858-2

Printed in Italy
010/110 REV

CONTENTS

• A (☞) in the text denotes a highly recommended sight

Athens

ATHENS AND
THE ATHENIANS

Mention the name Athens and almost everyone will have some preconceived ideas about the city. Socrates painted a picture with words in the fourth century B.C., Pausanais during the Roman era. In the 20th century, Hollywood added its own slant to the legends, and every school child learns about the gods of the ancient Greek world—of Zeus, Athena, and Apollo.

The most important city in the world during its heyday in the fifth and fourth centuries B.C., the people of Athens were highly sophisticated in their thoughts and actions, their tastes and fashions. This small city set on and around a dramatic hill of rock—the Acropolis—became the cradle of western civilization. From the public meetings held here the concepts of citizenship, democracy, and debate developed. Through their regard for learning, history and science were first codified and organized. The Athenian love of leisure allowed the development of numerous pursuits such as theater — imagine a world without tragedy or comedy (without the ancient Athenians, the much-loved TV soap opera might never have been possible). They also admired sporting prowess, inaugurating the Olympic Games where the best in the world would compete together simply for the glory of winning.

Athenians left an enduring legacy of concepts and ideas for humankind but they also bequeathed a remarkable number of buildings and artifacts that tell us about their lives. The remains of the temples of the Acropolis are recognized worldwide and hundreds of statues, along with ordinary household pottery, jewelry, and tools hold a fascination for anyone who enjoys exploring the past.

However, the city of Athens is more than a sum of these ancient parts. Though it disappeared from the record books following the decline of the Roman Empire in the fifth century—its lineage and magnificent monuments unappreciated—it has risen like a phoenix from the ashes since 1834, the year that it became capital of the modern country of Greece.

Grand buildings were erected to mark its re-birth. Though Neo-Classical design was fashionable everywhere in Europe in the mid-19th century, in Athens it echoed that of the original monuments of the ancient city—it was, in a sense, returning home. The elegant simplicity of the Parliament building, graceful façade of the University, and almost 'Rococo-esque' decoration on the Academy all hark back to ancient antecedents. Each was built with marble hewn from the Pentelic Hills just as those erected in Athens at the time of Socrates.

Visitors sit on the seats of an ancient amphitheater, reflecting on the thousands of events that have transpired here.

But there was a downside to this sudden re-emergence to center stage. People were drawn to the new capital like bees to a honey-pot, and throughout the 19th century the dispossessed of the economically floundering Aegean islands flocked here to find work. In the 1920s in the aftermath of WWII and the fall of the Ottoman Empire, Greece and Turkey agreed on a mass population swap, and millions of Greeks whose families had lived in Asia Minor (on the western Turkish coast) for generations, found themselves homeless in their spiritual homeland. Athens strained to accommodate many of them and a rash of building work saw the erection of the first faceless utilitarian suburbs that now surround the downtown area. Since buildings were kept low-rise in an attempt to make them earthquake proof, Athens began to spread outwards across the olive groves of nearby valleys. Not one of the world's prettiest cities, its preponderance for concrete can give it a drab and shabby look even on the brightest of days.

In the latter years of the 20th century very little was done to improve matters. The population grew but the infrastructure was not developed, resulting in gridlock of the urban traffic system, smog, and noise pollution. Today, at first glance nothing seems to have changed. A brown layer of pollution hangs over the city in both hot and cold weather; the seemingly endless hooting of horns down the wide boulevards and the drone of vehicles making painfully slow progress through the narrow streets raises noise levels; and in a city with so many apartments and so little parking it's no surprise that sidewalks become places to leave your vehicle, and pedestrians must risk life and limb by walking on the roads.

Perhaps this picture seems a little bleak, but there is one positive factor that eases the concern about visiting Athens. It's so easy to escape the city completely that one needn't feel trapped by the urban environment. Within an hour of being at Syntagma Square outside the National Parliament building (the symbolic heart of the city), you could easily be sitting at the quayside of some small Greek island having a cooling drink, or enjoying the pine forest of the countryside of Attica—the region that surrounds the capital.

Athenians understand this. They are not daunted or down-hearted by their surroundings, they enjoy their city, revelling in the opportunities it gives them. Every district has its own small squares with cafés, where people gather for a drink or meal—and Athenians love to eat out. You'll be surprised at the wealth of good restaurants offering international cuisine, and how much post-modernist décor influences interior design in the smarter districts. Of course the Greek taverna hasn't become extinct. Locals as much as visitors enjoy the fresh and delicious cuisine that's been served in Greece for centuries. Greek theater is thriving at new auditoria such as the Megaron complex, or at the open-air theaters on Lycabettus Hill. The annual Athens Festival has a full pro-gram of music, dance, and poetry with a rich historical lega-cy. Sports are still avidly followed, though today it's more likely to be football, not a discus throw, that excites the emo-tions. Powerboat racing out on the waters of the Saronic Gulf also raises the adrenalin of the wealthy.

Tradition still plays an important part in daily life here. The family forms the backbone of Greek society and filial ties are strong. Children play safely in the streets with grandma keeping a watchful eye. New babies are proudly shown to the world in the evening *volta* or stroll, when neighbors come to "bill and coo." Families gather for a weekend meal, taking over a corner of a tav-erna to spend a couple of hours in noisy debate (some may say argument) while perhaps having a little food. Eating always takes second place to conversation at a Greek meal. Greek hospitality is warm and genuine—even small examples such as always being welcomed with a smile and shown to your seats at a taverna. Shopkeepers are skilled salesmen, but never pushy or overbearing.

The Orthodox Church—for so long the one thing that united the Hellenic Diaspora—still has a strong influence on the population. Everyone from suited businessmen to young soldiers on national service make a regular visit to Athens Cathedral or a small local church to light a candle. People stop in on the way home from work or in their lunch breaks; it's such a nor-

An evening in a colorful Greek taverna is the best way to experience local life.

mal part of everyday life here. The Greek language also unifies the congregation with the clergy and Greeks around the world, though its use gives the capital a decidedly exotic air as visitors struggle to make sense of these "foreign" letters. There's also a sense of patriotism and national pride here even among the young—perhaps brought about by political upheavals in the late 20th century. Since Greek democracy was restored in 1975, after the military dictatorship, it is as though the population relish their country all the more.

However, since joining the European Union (then the Common Market) in 1981, Greece has definitely moved closer to her western cousins, being one of the first wave of countries to join the Euro currency zone. The government in

Athens has done well out of her union, receiving billions of dollars in aid, which has been used to upgrade vital road links throughout the country. Though the economy is still troubled, you are just as likely to see mobile phones as worry beads in a man's hand, and the young wear the latest European fashions just as the Italians and French do.

Tourism also continues to flourish at the dawn of the 21st century. It is Greece's major foreign currency earner with 11 million people visiting every year. Athens is an international melting pot with people of many nationalities treading the marble steps of the Acropolis to gaze at the birthplace of Western civilization. In 2004 the Olympic Games, first held in Greece during ancient times, will return to the capital giving Athens the chance to stand in the limelight again. The city offers some of the most fascinating and alluring archaeological remains in the world, yet those who visit in the 21st century find that the modern city works hard to live up to the past.

Visitors come to Greece for the history lesson, as well as for the scenic beauty and the festive entertainment.

A BRIEF HISTORY

In ancient Greek mythology Athens is named following a contest between Athena, goddess of wisdom, and Poseidon, god of the sea. Both had their eye on the prize real estate, so it was agreed that whoever could come up with the more useful gift for mortals would win. The half-human, half-serpent king of Athens, Cecrops, acted as arbiter.

First came Poseidon, who struck the rock of the Acropolis with his mighty trident and brought salt water gushing forth. Then it was Athena's turn. As she struck the rock an olive tree appeared, which proved more useful and valuable. Thus she acquired the position of the city's special protector.

The actual history of the city-state of Athens is just as fascinating as its mythology. From around 2000 B.C. wandering bands filtered into Greece from Asia Minor. Known as Achaeans, they were the first Greek-speaking people in the area, and over the centuries they built many imposing fortresses and developed the rich Mycenaean civilization, based in the Peloponnese. The citadel at Mycenae, seat of this most powerful of early Greek cultures, was erected to the south of Athens. Surrounded by a pair of precipitous ravines, the imposing walls of the citadel were some forty feet high and twenty feet thick, virtually impregnable.

The Achaeans' chief rivals and mentors were the dazzling Minoans of Crete—until about 1450 B.C., when the Minoan empire was devastated, possibly by tidal waves caused by the eruption of the volcanic island of Thera (Santorini). From the seafaring Minoans, the Myceneans learned to make bronze by combining copper and tin and, with no written language of their own, they adpated the linear script used by Minoan scribes. For several centuries, the Mycenaeans dominated the eastern Mediterranean and Aegean. A long series of conflicts, however, in-

The Theatre of Dionysus sits in the shadow of the great hill of the Acropolis.

cluding the legendary siege of Troy, weakened these mighty mainland warriors.

Around 1100 B.C. waves of Dorians swept into the area on horseback. Armed with iron spears and shields, they overpowered the Bronze Age weapons of Mycenae and broke down the Peloponnesian bastions. The ensuing "dark age" lasted about three centuries and resulted in large-scale emigrations of Greeks around the Mediterranean.

Athens managed to escape the scourge, but only after 700 B.C. did it take over and lift to unimagined heights the heritage of Mycenae and Crete. Although they warred as often as they united, the citizens of Athens and surrounding city-states on the Attica peninsula, notably Sparta and Thebes, shared a sense of identity. They were all Greeks — they had a common tongue and an evolving pan-Hellenic religion, and at regular intervals they were brought together by the ritual athletic contest of the Olympian, Delphian, and Isthmian games.

Athens, the largest city-state, gradually embraced all of the Attica peninsula. King Theseus, the legendary ruler who slew the minotaur in the Cretan labyrinth, was revered by Athenians for bringing Attica's scattered and independent villages under the rule of the Acropolis. Countless urns and jars were decorated with drawings of his heroic exploits, but in fact he belongs to myth rather than to history. The villages actually merged with Athens in exchange for protection, a share of state offices, and full citizenship rights.

From Aristocracy to Democracy

During the dark ages Athens had been a monarchy, but it emerged as an oligarchy in the seventh century B.C. The first great historical figure of that new era was Solon—general, merchant, poet, and sage—who in 594 B.C. became chief magistrate. At that time, civil war threatened to break out between the city-state's "haves" and "have nots" (an expression from ancient Greece). Armed with almost absolute powers, Solon produced a constitution advancing the ideal of equality before the law for citizens of all classes, set up a trial-by-jury system, freed the peasantry from debt to landowners, and introduced far-sighted reforms that revived the languishing economy.

In the middle of the sixth century, Athens' first dictator took power. Peisistratus established a dynasty that remained in uninterrupted power for half a century. On one occasion when he was forced from power, Peisistratus dressed a tall, beautiful country girl to look like the goddess Athena, and

Divine Dozen

Confused about the plethora of gods that ruled the heavens of ancient Greece? Here is a rundown of the main protagonists and their earthly responsibilities.

Zeus. Supreme ruler of the gods and men, protector of Greece, master of the weather; his symbols are the eagle and the oak tree. **Hera**. Zeus' third and oft-betrayed wife; protectress of marriage, mothers, and the home. **Athena**. Daughter of Zeus; goddess of wisdom; guardian of war heroes, who reputedly invented the flute and the potter's wheel; guardian of Athens. **Apollo**. Son of Zeus; god of the sun, music, healing, and prophecy (his advice was sought at the oracle of Delphi). **Artemis**. Twin sister of Apollo; goddess of hunting and the moon; guardian of women and cities. **Hermes**. Son of Zeus; messenger of the gods, the god of commerce, orators, and writers; protector of flocks, thieves, and travelers. **Ares**. Son of Zeus; god of war; unpopular on Olympus and feared by the Greeks. **Hephaestus**. Son of Zeus; god of fire and industry; the lame blacksmith of the gods who supplied Zeus with thunderbolts. **Aphrodite**. Daughter of Zeus; goddess of love, beauty, and gardens; the most beautiful goddess of Olympus. **Poseidon**. Zeus' brother; god of seas, rivers, and earthquakes, who caused storms with his trident and moved to an undersea Aegean palace when defeated by Zeus for control of the sky; giver of horses to man. **Demeter**. Sister of Zeus; goddess of agriculture; protectress of crops; gave men corn and the plow. **Hestia**. Zeus' elder sister; beloved goddess of fire and the hearth; protectress of the home, family, and city.

Other notable gods are **Dionysus**, Zeus' son by a mortal, god of wine, revelry, and hospitality; **Asklepios**, Apollo's son, god of healing; and **Hades**, ruler of the kingdom of the dead.

then entered Athens in triumph with the "goddess" leading his procession. Peisistratus, a resourceful and relatively benign tyrant, continued to steer Athens towards greatness. Under his rule, commerce and the arts flourished: Attica's wine and olive oil were shipped to Italy, Egypt, and Asia Minor in beautiful black-figure pots; the first tragedies ever written were performed at the annual festival of the wine god, Dionysus; and the standard version of Homer's works was set down.

However, Peisistratus' successors proved less popular, and democracy was eventually re-established by force. Cleisthenes, recognized by history as the true founder of Athenian democracy, took over in 508 B.C. An aristocrat by birth, he introduced electoral constituencies called *demes* and set up a sovereign citizens' assembly and a senate, whose members were chosen by lot. The foundations of representation had truly been set. He also introduced an inspired system of "ostracism" under which any public servant who was voted inept, tyrannical, or corrupt by the citizenry was banished from Athens for ten years, though he was allowed to keep his property.

The Persian Wars

At the end of the fifth century B.C., Greece entered the period of the Persian Wars, as recorded in Herodotus' great narrative history of the ancient world (see page 33).

The Persian Empire's far-flung lands included a number of Greek settlements on the coast of what is now Turkey. When the Greek towns attempted a revolt in 499 B.C., Athens sent an expedition to aid their uprising. The revolt failed, but the Persian king, Darius, could not let such impudence go unpunished, and in 490 B.C. he confidently launched an invasion of Attica. Although the Persians' forces and resources were vastly superior, Darius hadn't anticipated the amazing courage and battlefield skill of the Greeks.

A fleet of around 600 Persian vessels landed troops at Marathon beach. Led by General Miltiades, the Athenians inflicted a crippling and humiliating defeat on the Persians. According to legend, the soldier who ran from Marathon to Athens — a distance of 42 km (26 miles) — to report the victory then died of exhaustion. His feat is still commemorated today in the Olympic race known as the marathon.

However, the Persians still held a grudge and when Darius' son, Xerxes, re-invaded Greece by land and sea in far greater strength ten years later, the Greeks' defeat seemed inevitable. A few hundred heroic troops under Leonidas of Sparta delayed the enormous Persian army at the pass of Thermopylae long enough for the Athenians to be evacuated to the island of Salamis. When he finally arrived, Xerxes plundered the city, burning down all the wooden structures on the Acropolis.

The fleet of 700 Persian ships then engaged the much smaller Athenian naval force under the command of Themistocles in the Strait of Salamis, but Xerxes was in for a surprise. With the aid of brilliant tactics and newer ships, the Greek fleet trounced the Persians, turning the tide in favor of Athens. The final, decisive battle of the Persian Wars took place in 480 B.C. at Platae, where Xerxes' troops were soundly beaten. Greek independence had been preserved again, and with it the foundations on which Western civilization has been built.

The Golden Age

For almost 50 years after Platae, peace reigned at home, and the victorious city-state entered its most brilliant era. Athens was instrumental in bringing the disparate Aegean and mainland communities together, creating a "league of nations", known as the Delian League. The headquarters of the League was originally on the island of Delos but it was moved to Athens itself in 454 B.C. The resources of the treasury of the Delian League were used — among other things — to build the Parthenon and other monuments that still adorn the Acropolis today.

The moving power behind this unrivaled time of greatness, which has come to be known as the Golden Age, was Pericles. This liberal-inclined aristocrat was, in effect, the supreme ruler of Athens and its empire for 30 years until his death in 429 B.C.

Great works of art, literature, science, and philosophy were produced by what Pericles referred to as the "school of Hellas." Major names of the time included the dramatists Euripides and Sophocles, the historian Herodotus, the philosopher Socrates, and the brilliant scientists Zeno and Anaxagoras. The first literary salon in history was

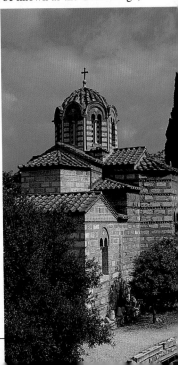

The church of the Holy Disciples is a remnant of the Byzantine Empire.

presided over by Aspasia, Pericles' mistress, a remarkable woman of intelligence and spirit.

During all this, the Athenian political system allowed the average citizen a greater degree of participation in public life than ever before anywhere, and perhaps since. Of course, the number of citizens (free adult males) was small—probably not above 30,000—while the population as a whole, including women, children, resident aliens, and slaves, might have been ten times as great.

Slavery was common, justified on the grounds that democracy could not exist unless the citizens were free to devote themselves to the service of the state. Most slaves in Athens were prisoners of war.

The Peloponnesian War

As Athens prospered, intense economic and ideological rivalry developed with Athens' ally during the Persian Wars, Sparta. In 431 B.C. the Peloponnesian War broke out between them resulting in 27 years of debilitating conflict, involving most of the Greek world. Yet literature and art continued to flourish in spite of the incessant fighting, and during this time Athens built two of the loveliest temples on the Acropolis, the Erechtheion and the temple to Athena Nike (see pages 34 and 35).

Finally, Sparta, with naval help from former foe Persia, blockaded what was then the Hellespont (now the Dardanelles Strait), thus cutting off Athens from its crucial supply of grain. Starvation and heavy naval losses proved too much for Athens, and the Spartans claimed total victory.

Sparta attempted to govern the city through a council of 30 men, known as the "Thirty Tyrants," who spent most of their time persecuting opponents and confiscating property. In less than a year they were driven from the city, and Sparta, embroiled in other conflicts, let Athens re-establish its maritime alliances without resistance.

But Athens was never to regain her earlier military or political influence. A new star rose in the north — that of Philip II of Macedon, father of Alexander the Great. He advanced the far-sighted scheme of a federation of Greek states, which Athens resisted. Some Athenians even urged the Assembly to declare war on the Macedonian King. (The fiery Philippics, speeches on the subject by master orator Demosthenes, rate among the finest of their kind.) Following defeat at the battle of Chaeronea in 338 B.C., however, the Athenians accepted an alliance with other states and even sent Philip a gold crown as a token of submission.

Yet culturally and intellectually Athens still remained unsurpassed through the fourth century B.C. Aristotle, one of the world's greatest philosophers, held forth at his own school of the Lyceum; Menander wrote comic plays; Praxiteles sculpted scores of superb statues, including that of Hermes, one of the greatest Greek sculptures, now in the museum at Olympia. This age, in fact, had an even more lasting influence than that exerted by Athens during its great "Classical" fifth century. Rome and Byzantium looked to it for inspiration, as Europe did in the Medieval and Renaissance periods.

Roman Rule

As the center of power shifted from Athens to Alexandria, Macedonian troops occupied Athens twice—first in 322 and then in 262 B.C. However, the Macedonian Empire did not survive long after Alexander's death. Eventually, after a series of wars, it was dismantled by the far-ranging legions of Rome. Macedonia became just another Roman province (in 146 B.C.) and Athens not much more than a showplace muse-

um city, though its philosophy schools and orators kept attracting Romans with political ambitions. Cicero and Horace spent student years in Athens, and Emperor Hadrian is said to have been initiated into the sacred mysteries of Demeter at Eleusis (the most famous secret religious rites of ancient Greece; see page 74).

Although generally treated well throughout some five centuries of Pax Romana, Athens suffered severely on one occasion. In 86 B.C., Roman general Sulla sacked the city in retribution for its unwise alliance with Mithridates, King of Pontus and bitter enemy of Rome. Many Athenian treasures were carried off to Italy.

Athens' good fortune was that the Romans held Greek culture in such high esteem. Most notable was the Emperor Hadrian (A.D. 76–138), who

The city of Athens is a vast array of the old and the new that changes with every year.

had a love of Classical Greek architecture. Among other monuments, he erected his distinctive arched gate, and completed the temple of Olympian Zeus on foundations laid by Peisistratus nearly seven centuries earlier (see page 57).

Byzantine and Ottoman Obscurity

When Roman Emperor Constantine gave Christianity official sanction in 326, he looked for a "New Rome" in the eastern Mediterranean. Athens hoped to be chosen but the title of new capital went to the former Greek colonial town of Byzantium (Constantinople), now Istanbul. Under Byzantine rule the city of Pericles sank into deep provincial obscurity. It merited only a few brief mentions in the history of the following centuries.

Christianity had taken early root in Greece, as a result of St. Paul's visit to Athens somewhere around 50 A.D. Polytheism, however, persisted until 529, when an edict by Emperor Justinian outlawed the last "pagan" temples and closed the famous Athenian schools of philosophy.

From the 12th to 14th centuries Athens found itself governed by a number of European nobles from Florence, Catalonia, and Burgundy. In 1456 Athens and Attica were taken by the Turks in their rampage across the disintegrating Byzantine Empire. The following four centuries of Ottoman rule are known as Greece's darkest age. Athens was all but forgotten. Through this difficult period, only the Orthodox Church could provide the Greek people with any sense of identity and continuity.

Venetian forces attempted to wrest the city from Ottoman control twice. The second time, in 1687, a shell hit a munitions store in the Parthenon—badly damaging the 2,000-year-old structure.

Independence

Athens dwindled ever further. When the poet Byron visited it in 1809, he found that what had once been the glittering center of the civilized world now had a population of only about 5,000 souls.

As the nineteenth century commenced, a swell of nationalist fervor rose in the oppressed people of Greece. On 25 March 1821, Archbishop Germanos raised a new blue-and-white banner in Patras in the Peloponnese and declared independence, but it took 11 years and some formidable foreign help for the Greeks to win their war against Turkish rule. Athens changed hands more than once during the long struggle in which many English, Scots, Irish, and French fought alongside the Greeks. Byron, who popularized the cause abroad, died at Missolonghi in 1824 (of disease, not from fighting).

On 27 October 1827, the Greek revolution was won, but the last Turks weren't evicted from the Acropolis until 1833. The following year, the little town of Athens was declared the capital of modern Greece.

Theoretically sovereign, the new state was an artificial creation—the result of pressure from other European powers—and the 17-year-old Bavarian Prince Otto was installed as king. He was deposed in 1862, but during his reign Athens slowly returned to being a city again, and Greece made considerable economic progress.

As a result of complex European diplomatic talks, a second adolescent came to the Greek throne in 1863, the 18-year-old William of the Danish royal house Schleswig-Holstein-Sonderburg-Glückburg. He took the name George I, King of the Hellenes, and remained in power for 50 years until his assassination in 1913.

The 20th Century

The events that have shaped modern Greek history have been as interesting and chaotic as any in the Classical age. The dominant figure between 1910 and 1935 was Eleftherios Venizelos, a Cretan politician who was prime minister several times. He helped Greece regain Macedonia and many of the Aegean islands, including his homeland of Crete. Venizelos was in power during the epic population exchange with Turkey (1922), under which almost one million repatriated Greeks flooded Athens. The desperate, makeshift effort to accommodate them pushed back the city's boundaries and accounts for the oldest of the suburban eyesores in the capital.

Between 1936 and 1940 Greece was under the military dictatorship of Ioannis Metaxas, remembered for the resounding *óchi* ("no") he gave in reply to Mussolini's ultimatum to surrender in 1940. The Greeks commemorate the day, 28 October, as a national holiday.

Greece was invaded by Nazi Germany in April 1941; by June the Germans controlled the entire country, with Italian forces placed in Athens. The people suffered greatly, but the city's monuments escaped serious damage. Unfortunately, the Greek resistance movement formed during the war was so politically divided that the guerrillas expended almost as much energy fighting each other as against the Germans. In October 1944, the Allied forces moved into Athens and much of Greece, encountering little opposition from the retreating Germans.

The war left Greece utterly devastated, and the factions squabbled ceaselessly in an attempt to gain political advantage. Communist and royalist partisans moved steadily toward a military confrontation as the United States, under the Truman Doctrine, sent the first economic aid. Two years of savage civil war ended in late 1949 with Communist defeat, but political instability persisted.

In 1967 a military dictatorship seized power in Greece. During the seven-year "reign of the colonels," as the succeeding years are known, political parties were dissolved, the press was censored, and left-wing sympathizers were exiled, tortured, and imprisoned. In November 1973 a student protest at the Athens Polytechnic was brutally crushed. This action spelled the end of public tolerance of the regime, which collapsed eight months later when the junta attempted to overthrow the Cypriot president, Archbishop Makarios, provoking the Turkish invasion of Cyprus. Constantine Karamanlis, the former conservative premier, was recalled from exile in Paris to restore democracy. The reforms that followed brought the abolition of the monarchy, and a new constitution for a republican government was drawn up in 1975.

With its entry into the Common Market in 1981, Greece's economic prospects strengthened. That same year, the first socialist government swept to victory under the leadership of Andréas Papandréou and the PASOK party. Papandréou espoused the desires of a post-war generation to maintain peace and stability, and to secure a better future for their children. By 1990, beleaguered by personal and financial scandals in the administration, PASOK was defeated at the polls after three rounds of voting, by the conservative New Democracy Party; Constantine Mitsotákis became the new prime minister. But the tenacious Papandréou was re-elected in 1994. He died in office in 1996, and was succeeded by Prime Minister Simitos who still holds the post.

In the 1990s Athens was awarded the 2004 Olympic Games. This, and Greece's agreement to join the Euro currency zone in 2002, has resulted in a great deal of infrastructure and economic development, which has not been without its problems. Traffic in the city is still in gridlock, stadium construction is behind schedule, and the Greek economy has yet to meet the requirements for monetary union, but government rhetoric is upbeat as both deadlines approach. The history of Athens reflects the ingenuity and vigor of the Greek spirit that will, no doubt, meet whatever challenges the modern world has in store for it.

HISTORICAL LANDMARKS

1100–800 B.C.	The Dark Age.
776–480 B.C.	The Archaic Period.
621–593 B.C.	Draco and Solon codify Athenian laws.
508 B.C.	Cleisthenes introduces democracy in Athens.
490 B.C.	First Persian War. Greeks succeed at Marathon.
480–338 B.C.	The Classical Period.
480 B.C.	Athens defeats the Persians in the Strait of Salamis.
477 B.C.	Athens unites allies under the League of Delos.
459–429 B.C.	The Golden Age of Pericles.
447–438 B.C.	The Parthenon is built on the Acropolis.
431–404 B.C.	Peloponnesian War; Sparta defeats Athens.
338–146 B.C.	The Hellenistic Period.
338 B.C.	Philip II of Macedon defeats the Athenians.
336–323 B.C.	Alexander the Great rules Greece.
149–146 B.C.	Greece falls under Roman rule.
A.D. 50	St. Paul brings Christianity to Athens.
A.D. 128	Emperor Hadrian rebuilds Athens.
A.D. 324	Constantinople becomes the capital of the Eastern Empire.
1456	Athens falls to the Turks.
1821–32	Greek War of Independence.
1833	Athens becomes the capital of Greece.
1922	Repatriated Greeks flood into Athens.
1941–44	Nazi Germany occupies Greece.
1944–49	Greek Civil War ends with Communist defeat.
1951	Greece becomes a member of NATO.
1967–74	Military junta rules Greece.
1981	Greece joins the Common Market.
1996	Prime Minister Papandréou dies.
2001	Greece becomes a member of the European Monetary Union
2004	Athens to host the Olympic Games.

WHERE TO GO

Viewed from the air—or from the high ground of the Acropolis or Mount Lycabettus—Athens is a sprawling city; a maze of apartment blocks and office buildings stretching as far as the eye can see. Yet the downtown area is remarkably compact. Most of the major sites are within walking distance of one another, but the inexpensive and reliable Metro system links many museums and attractions for those who get a little foot weary.

Ancient remains are scattered across the central downtown area and Athens has grown almost organically throughout its history, resulting in numerous districts, each with its own particular character. This guide divides the city into a number of sections, covering the ancient center of the city first and then moving clockwise through the other important districts. Attractions featured will include major squares, gardens, ruins, monuments, and museums.

The heart of ancient Athens was centered around the dome of the Acropolis, with sacred temples built atop the rock and the town built on its undulating flanks. Today the area is still replete with Greek and Roman remains, though these are interspersed with later buildings—a fascinating mixture of Neo-Classical mansions and terraced cottages dating back to Ottoman times. This area, known as Plaka, is now perhaps the most charming in Athens and acts as a magnet to visitors from around the world.

 ## THE ACROPOLIS

It is impossible to overestimate the importance of the Acropolis to the ancient Greeks. The religious significance of this sheer-sided rock, 90 m (300 ft) above the town, was paramount, and the enduring images of the temples there still represent the principles of freedom and democracy in the present day. You can see the temples from most parts of the city—particularly at night when they are well-lit—which only adds to the feeling that this small area is still the essence of the city. The name Acropolis derives from the Greek words *acro* meaning "highest point" and *polis*, meaning town.

Try to visit early or late in the day to avoid the tour groups, or on Mondays, when most tours don't operate; and remember to wear comfortable, flat shoes as there are many slippery stones worn smooth over the centuries, and numerous uneven areas where heels can catch.

Once through the ticket office a path leads to the summit of the Acropolis—a relatively flat plateau around 320 m by 130 m (1,049 ft by 426 ft) in area. This path is the original "sacred way," used for ceremonial entrances to the inner sanctum in ancient times.

Used for strategic purposes throughout the Mycenaean and Archaic periods the rock was easy to defend; it had a water supply and superb views of the surrounding area. The first religious structures appeared at the end of the sixth century B.C., when the summit became a sanctuary and the town was founded on lower ground below. These early temples were destroyed by the Persian forces of Xerxes in 480 B.C. Following this, new defensive walls were constructed that included elements of the ruined old Temple of Athena and the old Parthenon.

It was during the era of Pericles that construction began on many of the buildings that we see today. He commissioned the Parthenon, Erechtheíon, Temple of Athena Nike, and Propylaia, taking advantage of a new marble quarry on Mount Pentelikon—the marble became known as Pentelic. As the Romans took control of Athens they embellished the

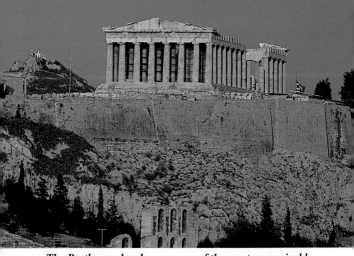

The Parthenon has become one of the most recognizable structures in the world—it is a symbol of the ancients.

site with small additions, but the wake of Christianity and the decline of Roman power saw the Acropolis vulnerable to attack, theft, and vandalism. Statuary was removed and temples were used as palaces by European nobles during the 14th century. The rock reverted to its earliest use as a strategic stronghold during Ottoman rule, resulting in damage to most of the major structures. Vast amounts of stone were taken from temples on the pinnacle for a program of building in the city below.

Following Greek independence, a zealous restoration project saw the removal of all medieval and Ottoman structures on the plateau, and harkened the beginning of archaeological study of the ancient remains. This continues to the present day.

First impressions as you make your way towards the inner sanctuary are of the **Beulé Gate**, a Roman addition of the third century A.D. The path leads on directly in front of the Temple of Athena Nike to the **Propylaia** (sacred entrance-way), which led on into the inner sanctum. This monumental gateway was a sign of things to come, and for the ordinary citizens of Athens it was meant to inspire and impress. It retains this ability in modern times, even though the structure was never finished. Construction began in 437 B.C. to a plan by Mnisikles, an otherwise unknown architect. A series of six Doric columns mark the transition into the Propylaia following which there are four symmetrical rooms, two on either side of the walkway. Ionic colonnades frame the walkway (this was the first building to incorporate both styles of column). There were five heavy wooden doors along the walkway, heightening the tension of those ancient pilgrims, as each would be opened in turn. The only room to have been completed was the second on the northern side. This was used as a waiting room and also, according to the Roman historian Pausanias, as a picture gallery or **Pinakotheke**, the name it holds today.

Once through the Propylaia, the sacred way leads on to the Acropolis plateau proper. In Classical times a 9 m (30 ft) statue of Athena Promachos (the Defender) dedicated to Athenian exploits during the Persian Wars stood immediately beyond the entranceway. This was taken to Constantinople during the Byzantine era. Make your way left along the southern flank of the Propylaia to view the **Temple of Athena Nike** (Athena of Victory). The Acropolis had been a sanctuary to Athena Nike since the fifth century B.C. and following the sacking of the site by the Persians a new smaller temple, or *naïskos,* was commissioned and designed by Callicrates. Six elegant columns support a pediment with decorative friezes depicting the gods on Mount Olympus and heroic battle scenes of Greek warriors fighting barbarians. The temple, built on the remains of an older Mycenaean wall, offers excellent views across the surrounding landscape, and this location was prized by the Ottomans, who tore down the structure to build a defensive battery. The temple has been painstakingly re-erected using rubble found underneath the battery when it was removed in the 1830s.

Walking back to the center of the plateau you'll pass scant remains of the **Sanctuary of Artemis Brauronia** founded in the fourth century B.C., but your eyes will be drawn to the immense structure of the Parthenon, which dominates today's Acropolis site.

The Parthenon

The Parthenon is one of the most recognizable buildings in the world. The series of columns supporting pediment and frieze is Athens to many visitors, and would have been also to travelers in ancient times. However, they would have seen a structure with a veneer of splendid color and decorated with magnificently carved sculptures; not to mention a strong wooden roof now lost to posterity. What remains is the bare Pentelic marble used in the construction and the refined lines and form that make it an architectural masterpiece.

The Parthenon was dedicated to Athena and means Temple of the Virgin—Athena in her guise as protector of the city, goddess of wisdom and justice. It also housed the national treasury, bringing together the spiritual and secular power of ancient Greece. At least four other Parthenons have been built on the site—in fact, the base of the present temple indicates that its predecessor was wider. Designed by architects Callicrates and Iktinus, work began in 447 B.C. and the temple was dedicated in 438 B.C. with a huge celebration, the Panathenaic Festival, that involved thousands of people; live animals were sacrificed at an altar on the eastern façade. This festival then took place every four years during the Pagan era and continued until the fifth century A.D. (see page 42). Converted into a church in the sixth century, the *cella* (inner temple) had frescoes painted on its walls and upper galleries where women worshipped. A bell tower was added by the Byzantines who named it Agia Sophia, also meaning wisdom. Later, under Ottoman rule, the bell tower became a minaret and the church was converted into a mosque.

A Greek "Who's Who"

In a city with the pedigree of Athens—the cradle of democracy, history, philosophy, drama, and comedy—it is not surprising that it was the birthplace of some of the most illustrious figures in history. Here are just a few.

Socrates (c469–399 B.C.)—philosopher and orator who pursued truth through dialectic discourse.

Plato (c428–347 B.C.)—student of Socrates; political and religious philosopher; founded his own academy of higher study.

Aristotle (384–322 B.C.)—philosopher; student at Plato's academy and tutor to Alexander the Great.

Herodotus (484–425 B.C.)—"father of history," who wrote thorough accounts of the conflicts of the early Persian wars.

Thucydides (c460–400 B.C.)—established an analytic methodology for recording history. Chronicled the Peloponnesian War.

Callicrates and **Iktinos**—architects of the Parthenon and other great buildings in the ancient city.

Phidias and **Praxiteles**—sculptors who adorned these buildings with graceful statues, friezes, and ornate pediments.

Sophocles and **Aeschylus**—great tragic poets.

Euripides (480–406 B.C.)—wrote tragedies based around ordinary mortal characters rather than the Greek gods.

Aristophanese (448–385 B.C.)—originator of the Greek comedy.

33

Eventually it was used as a powder magazine. In September 1687 Venetian forces threatened Athens and one of their mortars hit the Parthenon, igniting the powder inside. The resulting explosion badly damaged the structure and many other ancient buildings on the site. The center of the Parthenon was totally destroyed along with many columns and priceless carved friezes. Subsequent "licences" granted by the Ottomans to European nobles saw many prize friezes disappear to archaeological collections around Europe, including the Elgin marbles (ornately carved pediments) that were taken to London by Lord Elgin. Restoration of the temple has been almost constant since 1834.

Today it is not possible to walk among the columns and through what remains of the inner temple. This echoes the rules of ancient Greece, when only the highest priests could enter the *cella*. There they would be able to worship an ivory-and-gold-covered wooden statue of Athena said to be 12 m (39 ft) high which has long since been lost. Walk around the 70 m (228 ft) by 30 m (101 ft) exterior to really appreciate the grace of the columns. There are no straight lines anywhere in the building—the graduated curves simply create the illusion of the vertical and horizontal.

To the north of the Parthenon stand the graceful statues of the **Porch of the Caryatids**, which adorn the southern façade of the **Erechtheíon**. This temple is an unusual mélange of architectural styles, with rooms at varying levels, where the worship of three gods took place. It was the last of the great building flurry of Pericles to be finished, dedicated in 406 B.C. Built beside an ancient Temple of Athena whose scant remains can just be seen, the Erechtheíon brought together the worship of Athena and Poseidon under one roof—legend says that following the contest between the two gods for the honor of protecting Athens, they were reconciled and this dual temple recognized their special bond with regard to the city. Erechtheus — part man, part snake — was a legendary King of Athens who, over the generations, became closely connected with Poseidon. A temple of Zeus also forms part of the complex. The temple was damaged by fire almost immediately, and again during the Roman period. It was converted into a church in the sixth century A.D. and was used as a harem building during Ottoman times.

The caryatids — female figures used as pillars — are thought to represent the Arrephoroi (maidens who attended to the goddess Athena and performed rituals in the sanctuary and the temple), as they all originally carried libation vessels in their hands. Both the vessels and the arms of the caryatids have been destroyed. The sculptures at the site are copies, with all but one of the originals displayed in the Acropolis Museum. Their portico protected the tomb of Cecrops, the mythical founder of Athens.

Beyond the porch is the eastern façade. Here a row of Ionian columns mark the entrance to a rectangular inner sanctum of the new **Temple of Athena**. The walls of the interior were removed during the Byzantine era, and the north corner (column and pediment) was removed by

These statues decorate the Erechtheíon temple along the Porch of the Caryatids.

Elgin and taken to London with the "Elgin marbles."

A large north porch balances that of the southern Porch of the Caryatids. This sits on high foundations as the ground level falls steeply on the northern side. Much of the building here dates from the time of the Roman Empire—a devastating fire destroyed the earlier **temples to Zeus and Poseidon**. Marks on the ground in the porch area suggest that this building was once struck by lightning. A hole was left in the ceiling of the temple since the belief at the time was that a lightning strike should never be closed off from the sky. Ancient Greeks believed that the

This triple-headed demon is a prized display in the Acropolis Museum.

Acropolis was guarded by a giant snake that lived under this temple. Pilgrims would buy honey cakes for this snake and leave them at the temple entrance for it to enjoy.

The west wall was restored in the early 20th century after it fell down in 1852. The reconstruction recreates the temple of the Roman era.

The **Acropolis Museum** in the southeast corner of the plateau was opened in 1934. It was designed and built so as not to spoil the skyline or compete with the temples and it cannot be seen from the streets of the city or from the sacred way as you enter through the Propylaia. Much of the fine statuary and carved friezes still present when Ottoman forces left have been displayed here along with four of the original Caryatid statues from the Erechtheíon. The museum displays pieces of the ornate decorative pediment that adorned the temples, and dedications to Athena herself found in the inner sanctuary. The whole collection is breathtaking and proof if it were needed of the immense wealth and influence of this ancient site. Each room has something of note but look for the pediment of a lion tearing apart a bull, dating from the sixth century B.C. in room 1. Pediment depicting a triple-headed demon, and a *kouros* (male statue) named *The Calf-bearer*—a young man carrying a calf to ritual slaughter at the temple—are both displayed in room 2. *Kritikos Boy* and *Blond-haired Boy*—two sculptures carved in the "severe" style fashionable around 480 B.C. are displayed in room 6. Panels from the Ionic frieze that decorated the Parthenon are in room 8, and the original Caryatids can be found in room 9.

When you have explored the architectural delights of the Acropolis, take time to enjoy the views from its walls. Sections of the stone defences date back to Mycenaean times, though the majority were constructed during the first millennium and were reinforced by the Turks. From the north you can take in the other major archaeological sites and the district of Plaka directly below. From the east the verdant slopes of Mount Lycabettus come into view, with the smart district of Kolonaki on its lower slopes. South leads the eye towards the coast and the islands of the Saronic Gulf.

As you leave the site via the smooth stone path through the Propylaia you'll pass the **Monument of Agrippa**. Originally erected with a single chariot to commemorate victory in the Panathenaic Games, a second chariot group including Marcus Agrippa was added in 27 B.C. You'll leave through the Beulé Gate, a remaining part of the Roman defensive system.

AROUND THE ACROPOLIS

A number of other archaeological remains can be found on the flanks of the Acropolis and on nearby hills. Head south of the rock by taking a left out of the main entrance and you'll reach the first after a five-minute stroll.

The **Odeon of Herodes Atticus** was one of the last great building projects of ancient Athens. The vast auditorium was completed towards the end of the second century A.D. in typical Roman style. During Byzantine times it was used as a dye works, and the Ottomans used it for defensive purposes. However, excavations began in the 1850s and the Odeon is once again holding spectacular summer performances.

On the southeastern flank of the Acropolis are the vast remains of the **Theatre of Dionysus**, hacked out of the earth in the fifth century B.C. and upgraded in the third century B.C. In Roman times a long colonnaded *stoa* and promenade linked the two theaters, but only scant remains can be seen today. The theater (separate fee with entrance at Odós Thrasyllou) was the birthplace of the dramatic and comic art and formed the social and political heart of Athens during its "golden age." The premiers of several major pieces by Sophocles, Euripides, and Aristophanes were performed here, and the Athens assembly also met here late in its history. The whole auditorium held 17,000 people, but most interesting are the carved front row thrones for VIPs, including one with lion's-claw feet that was reserved for the priest Dionysus Eleutherios. The particularly fine **bema of Phaedros** (carved stage) depicting scenes from the life Dionysus—god of wine and merriment—is of Roman origin. Surrounding the theater are remains of several other buildings including an **Asclepieion** (place of healing) and

Odeon of Pericles. These are currently being worked on by archaeologists.

To the west of the Acropolis stands another small range of hills now cut by footpaths and covered in trees offering cooling shade in the heat of summer. This area, reached by crossing Odós Rovertou Gali and walking up behind the Dionysus restaurant, offers splendid views across to the Acropolis (it's the best place for afternoon overviews), and the Sound and Light Show auditorium is located here for this reason. Several archaeological sites can be seen and the area is much less crowded than the Acropolis itself. You'll also see the 16th century church, **Ayios Dimítrios Loumbardhi**, nestling under the woodland canopy.

In the northeastern area, you'll come to the **Hill of the Pnyx**, meeting place of the Assembly of Athens. Loosely translated, *pnyx* means "crowded or tightly packed place," and in ancient times this was a highly populated area. You'll

see the outlines of walls, including the defensive **Themistoklean Wall**, between the bushes or under the turf as you stroll. The Pnyx meeting place can be found below the summit on the northeastern side of the hill. When democracy was established at the end of the sixth century B.C. the debating chamber moved from

Listen to a concert on a summer evening at the ancient Odeon of Herodes.

the Agora to this structure and it was here that the great statesmen of Greece made their speeches at the rostrum. Seats were provided for the 5,000 citizens of the city needed for a decision-making quorum, who would listen to the arguments of Pericles and Themistocles.

On the **Hill of the Nymphs** north of the Pnyx you'll see the Neo-Classical lines of the original **Athens Observatory**, founded in 1842. Perhaps the most popular point for visitors lies in the south where at the highest point—Hill of the Muses or **Philopappos Hill**—is the **Tomb of Philopappos**, a high-ranking nobleman in Roman times. Its convex façade has a sculptured frieze depicting Julius Philopappos riding a chariot and performing his duties in the Senate. It is from here that you'll get the best views of the Acropolis, so don't forget your camera or video recorder!

On the north flank of the Acropolis is the hill of **Areopagos**, found close to the right of the main Acropolis ticket office. With views across the city below it is a popular spot for photographs, however it also has a long and illustrious history. Tradition states that this was the site of the original Agora of Athens, and the original council of the city was known as the Council of Areopagos. Later it held courts of law, and justice was dispensed here. In A.D. 51 St. Paul addressed a crowd of Athenians from the hill with his sermons of Christian faith. He met with a hostile response from the Pagan population, but did convert Dionysus who later became the patron saint of Athens.

PLAKA AND ANAFIOTIKA

After all the exploration of these fascinating archaeological sites, you'll probably be ready for a rest and change of scenery. As you make your way to the city you'll pass through two small districts which offer a range of cafés, bars, and tavernas, along with images of Greek daily life not found in more modern parts of Athens.

The tiny area called **Anafiotika** hugs the high ground immediately below the Acropolis. Built in the 19th century for migrant workers from around Greece that came to take advantage of construction opportunities in the capital, the first few families came from the island of Anafi and wanted to create surroundings that would remind them of home. Today the narrow lanes with their neat, whitewashed, cottages and plethora of potted geraniums are still reminiscent of the Aegean settlements across the water.

Plaka lies below Anafiotika and fills the space between the ancient and modern city, stretching to Odós Ermou and Syntagma Square to the north. This was the center of population from Byzantine times through to Greek independence, and thus can be called Athens Old Town. The maze of narrow—mostly traffic-free—streets is a delight to explore and there are numerous shops and eateries to choose from. Playful cats dart down the narrow alleyways, and you may be lucky to hear the Terpsichordean notes of the *laterna* drifting through the streets—these hand-turned barrel organs are now becoming extremely rare. Plaka is particularly atmospheric in the evenings when locals enjoy a *volta,* or stroll, before dinner and tavernas set tables out on the narrow side streets. It is almost a living museum with Byzantine Churches, Neo-Classical mansions housing galleries or collectibles stores, and a wealth of historical detail at every turn. Do look beyond the tempting shop fronts to really get the most out of your tour. Though you'll want to simply follow your nose around the district, here are the locations of the main historical attractions of Plaka.

At Kidathinéon 17 you'll find the **Museum of Greek Folk Art**, which offers an interesting collection of embroidery, lace, and numerous liturgical garments. Spinning and weaving is also highlighted along with traditional puppets and festival masks and costumes. The collection features artifacts from all over Greece and her islands. Other divisions of the folk art museum can be found around the city.

On the southern end of Odós Adrianou, in a small square surrounded by cafés, is the **Monument of Lysicrates**. Dating from the fourth century B.C., it consists of a series of curved panels and columns creating a circular structure supporting a dome made from a single block of Pentelic marble. Originally, this would have been topped by a bronze tripod —a prize awarded in choral competitions during the Classical era. In the 18th century a Capuchin monastery occupied land all around the monument and the interior of the base was used as a guest room. Lord Byron stayed here

---

The Panathenaic Festival

This important festival was made popular by Peisistratos (546–528 B.C.). It was held every four years in August, on the birthday of the goddess Athena.

The festivities comprised athletics contests, equestrian events, and musical extravaganzas and the winners were given vials containing olive oil from the fruit of the sacred trees of Athens. However, the most important element of the celebration was the procession that led from Kerameikos through the Agora, culminating at the Acropolis and the Temple of Athena, her main center of worship. At the head of the procession on a ship carried by priests and priestesses was an embroidered garment to adorn the statue of Athena herself. This had been woven by the female guardians of the temple—the Arrhephoroi.

Once within the temple, animal sacrifices were made before the statue was robed and the procession was disbanded; but no doubt the festivities continued, with a carnival atmosphere throughout the city for a number of days.

---

in 1810 and is said to have written some of his work while enjoying the seclusion.

One mansion on Odós Panós, high up near the Acropolis, has been turned into a museum. **The Kanellópoulos Museum**, which opened in 1976, has a family collection of artifacts from many eras of Athens' history. Mycenaean figurines and pottery, Classical Greek and Roman sculpture, and Byzantine icons, frescoes and tapestries are all well-displayed and illustrate very effectively the varied influences that make up the history of the city.

To the Greek and Roman Agoras

From Plaka there are numerous streets leading northwest towards the sites of the Roman and Greek Agoras, however the most direct route is via Odós Adrianou. Take a short diversion right along Odós Paleologolou to explore **Mitrópolis**, Cathedral of the City of Athens. Built in the 1840s following Greek independence from the remains of over 70 churches, it is now surrounded by a network of supporting scaffolding erected following damage sustained in the 1999 earthquake. The cathedral is a focus for prayer, particularly to the Black Madonna surrounded by an ornate silver frame. In the shadow of the cathedral is the tiny **Mikrí Mitrópolis** (Little Cathedral), officially named Panayía Gorgoepíkos and sometimes known as Ayios Eleuthérios or "freedom church," the name given after King Otto left the Greek throne. Dating from the 12th century, the church was built using stone from the ancient sites of the city. Wander around its exterior walls to see sections from Greek and Roman columns, or fragments of ornate pediments.

Nearby—where Mitropoleos meets Pentelis—is another church, **Ayía Dinamis**, which means "the holy power of the Virgin." This tiny place of worship has survived the redevelopment of the district but now sits literally underneath a modern office block.

When Adrianou meets Odós Eolou, it is cut by excavations on the site of **Hadrian's Library** (Adrianou once passed directly through the site and still continues on the other side). The site is closed to the public but can easily be viewed from the surrounding streets. Built in A.D. 123, only the western wall is in good order. Turn left along Eolou to find the site of the **Roman Agora**. Founded in the first century A.D. to accommodate an expanding Athens, the ornate entrance gate was commissioned by Julius Caesar in honor of Athena

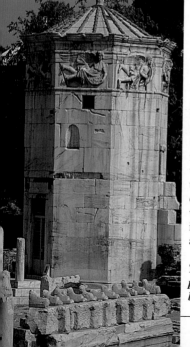

Archegetis (Founder of the City). Much of the north and west wall of the Agora lies unexcavated under the houses of Plaka, but the south wall and the remains of the south colonnade are there, along with a series of shops near the ticket office. The most remarkable building in the Agora complex (though it was outside the Agora when built) is the **Tower of the Winds**. This ornate octagonal-shaped structure was a clock and meteorological station built by astronomer Andronikos in

The Tower of the Winds was predicting the forecast long before the Weather Channel.

the first century B.C. Each of the eight faces corresponds to a cardinal point on the compass and is decorated with an ornate frieze depicting the wind blowing from that direction. The timing device was water-driven with a supply from the Acropolis above.

Just beside the Agora you'll see one of only two mosques still standing in the city—it now houses an archaeological workshop and is not open to the public. Nearby on Odós Diogenous is the **Museum of Greek Folk Music** with a fascinating collection of instruments and musical recordings bringing the varied regional folk music of Greece to life.

Continue along Adrianou to find the remains of the **Ancient Greek Agora**—birthplace of western democracy and the social heart of the ancient city-state of Athens (agora comes from the Greek *agiero*, meaning to assemble). From the sixth century B.C., this area played host to a number of activities including religious and political meetings, law courts, education, shopping, or simply passing the time of day. Here Socrates regaled the people with his philosophical theories—unfortunately for him he fell foul of the authorities and was put to death in 403 B.C. St. Paul met an audience of "skeptics" who argued against him when he gave a speech here in A.D. 51. The whole area was razed during Barbarian attacks in the centuries following the fall of the Roman Empire and was covered with new buildings during Byzantine times, all of which had to be cleared when excavations began.

From the entrance at Adrianou (there are two other entrances to the site) look immediately to your right to see remains of the **Altar of the Twelve Gods**; a small monument from where distances from Athens to all other points in the Greek world were measured. This was truly the center of the world during the Classical Greek era. Directly ahead in the area of the central Agora the outline of the **Altar of Ares** and **Temple of Ares** can be seen in gravel. Behind this, the remains of the **Odeon of Agrippa**, built in 15 B.C., and the Royal Palace overlaid by two later *stoas* can be discerned. In the southeast corner of the site, the 11th century church of **Ayios Apostoloi** is the only building on the site remaining from the Byzantine era. Greatly changed over the centuries it was fully restored to its original form in the late 1950s. The paintings in the narthex are original; others were transplanted from the Hephaisteion (see below) when it was deconsecrated.

To the right, facing the main square are two **Bouleuterions** (council chambers). These served the city from the time of Kleisthenes and his Council of 500 in the late fifth century B.C. Beyond the council chambers stands the best-preserved temple in Athens—the **Hephaisteion** or Temple of Hephaistos, also known as the Thisio. The design of the temple is classic Doric and was completed after the Persian invasions. Hephaistos was the god of metalworking, and this temple was set at the heart of the smithing and iron-mongery district of the city. Later it was converted into a church with the addition of interior walls and this survived through Ottoman times—the last services were performed in the 1830s. For some years following it served as the first archaeological museum in Greece.

The exterior of the temple is well-preserved and uses the same curved lines as the Parthenon, though the columns are more slender and the entablature (horizontal platform above the columns) sturdier. The *metopes* (carved space on a Doric frieze) around the entablature depict the legendary feats of Heracles and Theseus. Surrounding the temple is a garden area attempting to recreate a garden that existed here in the ancient era. It includes the same plants species—medicinal and herbal—that were popular during that time.

The eastern flank of the Agora site is dominated by the **Stoa of Attalos**. First erected by King Attalos of Pergamon and opened in 138 B.C., it was faithfully recreated during the 1950s to offer us a stunning vision of what communal buildings were like in ancient times. Stoas were extremely popular in the Roman era and all large settlements had one. These long porches or porticos provided shade in summer and shelter in winter and they were often used to link important community buildings. The Stoa of Attalos was a two-story construction with rooms at the back that housed

The beautiful re-creation of the porticoed Stoa of Attalos houses the Agora Museum.

small shops. Today it is home to the **Agora Museum** and displays numerous artifacts found at this extensive sight. Here you'll find a range of everyday objects not seen in the Acropolis Museum, in addition to religious and civic statuary and mosaics.

The route of the great "sacred way" that linked the Agora with the Acropolis above—and that was used during the Panathenaic Festival—is now being excavated and rebuilt to allow visitors to walk in the footsteps of the ancient Athenians.

Monastiráki and Thissio

The area immediately to the north of the Greek Agora— Monastiráki—is one of the most interesting in Athens. Under the Ottomans it held the main market and despite the great amount of archaeological excavation that has taken place since the 1820s, it still retains the atmosphere of an oriental bazaar. Its streets are full of small trinket shops, coffee shops, and bars. In a throwback to ancient times there is still a metalworking and blacksmith area that produces handmade items, and you can find textiles, ceramics, and copies of the latest "streetwear." Monastiráki is particularly cosmopolitan on Sundays when a huge flea market fills the streets and you can haggle over furniture and knick-knacks for that unique remembrance of your trip.

The district centers on **Monastiráki Square** (with its busy Metro station). The church at its heart—the **Pantánassa**— is thought to be part of a large monastery complex that sat here before the Ottoman invasion. As if to reiterate this historical event, the south side of the square is dominated by the **Mosque of Tsistarákis**, built in 1759 and named after the Ottoman governor of the time. It now houses the ceramics branch of the Museum of Greek Folk Art.

The main thoroughfare cutting through the district is Odós Ermou, which leads east to Syntagma Square (see page 55). Ermou is one of the main shopping streets of the city, and numerous European retailers have outlets here. A small square cuts its path just a little way from Monastiráki Square, and it is decorated with the beautiful Byzantine church of **Kapnikaréa**, the official church of Athens University. Built in the 11th century its dome is supported by four Roman columns and its modern frescoes were created in the 1950s by Fotis Kondoglou. Kapnikaréa was earmarked for demolition in the 1830s but was saved by the personal intervention of Prince Ludwig of Bavaria, father of Greece's first king.

The arched entry of an ancient mosque reflects Monastiráki's Ottoman past.

We'll take the route west from Monastiráki Square, as if leaving the city. This leads us one kilometer (.62 miles) to the archaeological site of **Kerameikós**. As you walk along, immediately to the north of Ermou (on your right) is the district of Psirí. Unspoiled by tourism, there is a very Greek atmosphere in the maze of narrow streets and some excellent tavernas among its traditional shops.

The excavated area of Kerameikós is interesting because it incorporates a section of the 478 B.C. city wall and the ceremonial entranceways into Athens from the cities of Eleusis to the west and Piraeus to the south. The Panathenian Festival Procession would start from here on its journey to the Acropolis, and the procession of the Eleusian Mysteries would leave from here through the **Sacred Gate** and along the **Sacred Way**. The most important building found here is the **Pompeion**, where procession paraphernalia was stored and where those involved in major processions would ready themselves.

Kerameikós was named for the potters who worked here within the city walls (Inner Kerameikós), directly on the site of good clay deposits. Their work was carried around the Greek empire and is now displayed in museums worldwide, but they were not highly regarded by citizens in ancient times. Outside the wall (Outer Kerameikós), was the major cemetery of the city (it was forbidden to bury the dead within the city walls), with burials dating from the 12th century B.C. Major figures from Greek history, including Pericles, were buried here and their funerary artifacts are some of the most exquisite items found during excavations around the city. A small museum has burial finds dating from 12th–sixth centuries B.C. but you'll see many more in the National Archaeological Museum.

> Take a nap in the afternoon—to allow you to enjoy the long evenings.

For those whose taste leans towards post-industrial landscapes, just a little way beyond Kerameikós—across Odós Pireos—is the old gas works of Gazi, which has been converted into the **Museum of Industrial Architecture**. It also hosts a regular program of art and photography exhibitions.

Omonia Square (Plateìa Omónias)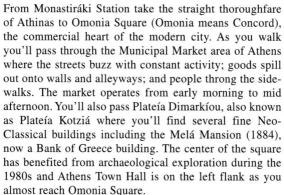

From Monastiráki Station take the straight thoroughfare
of Athinas to Omonia Square (Omonia means Concord),
the commercial heart of the modern city. As you walk
you'll pass through the Municipal Market area of Athens
where the streets buzz with constant activity; goods spill
out onto walls and alleyways; and people throng the sidewalks. The market operates from early morning to mid
afternoon. You'll also pass Plateía Dimarkíou, also known
as Plateía Kotziá where you'll find several fine Neo-
Classical buildings including the Melá Mansion (1884),
now a Bank of Greece building. The center of the square
has benefited from archaeological exploration during the
1980s and Athens Town Hall is on the left flank as you
almost reach Omonia Square.

The rather shabby modern buildings belie Omonia's importance. It's always busy with people; there are some good
cafés and restaurants, and some of the most prestigious companies have offices here. Combine this with the bus and Metro
routes that run through it, and you have a major city hub.

The National Archaeological Museum

A ten-minute walk north of the square on Odós Patission is
the **National Archaeological Museum**, one of the most
prestigious archaeological collections in the world. Finds
cover 7,000 years of Greek history, and have been brought
from sites all across Greece. The collection brings the
ancient Greek world to life shedding light on almost every
aspect of the daily activities of the citizens. Prepare to
spend at least two hours here, don't try and rush this amazing collection. The map of the museum issued with your
ticket will be a great help in finding your way around the
somewhat confusing array of rooms and corridors. You are

sure to find your own favorites, but here are a few acknowl-
edged highlights.

In the prehistoric collection (rooms 3–6) enjoy the treasure-trove found at Mycenae, including the exquisite, gold
Mask of Agamemnon. Schiemann thought that this was
placed over the face of the dead King Agamemnon around
1200 B.C., but in fact it dates from over 300 years earlier; the
prehistoric rooms also have a collection of Cycladic figures
dating from the third millennium B.C. The simple, rounded
female figures were funerary or religious objects and are in
total contrast to the intricate pediment and frieze carvings
and religious statuary found at temples on the Acropolis and
in the Acropolis Museum. You'll also see a rare male figure
among the collection, and the beautiful *Harp Player*—a
more complex carving in the same style.

Rooms 7–35 concentrate on sculpture—perhaps the
greatest collection of ancient sculpture in the world—and
these are displayed to show the chronological development
of the art form. Simply styled male and female figures
(*kouros* and *kore*) of the Achaiac Age (seventh–fifth century
B.C.) give way to more ornate and literal human forms as you
walk through the collection into the Classical Age and then
on to the Hellenistic and Roman eras. Greek gods are popular themes, followed by eminent human figures of Roman
times. Room 7 holds the important early statue of Artemis by
Nikandre of Naxos (c640 B.C.).

Room 15 is dominated by a fine statue of Poseidon in bronze
(460 B.C.) found in the sea off the island of Euboea. The god
is set to launch his trident against foes unknown. The Hall of
the Stairs hosts another statue dredged from the sea, that of the
Jockey of the Artemision. The diminutive jockey drives on the
handsome steed which has its two front legs raised into the air,
as if about to leap over an invisible obstacle.

The golden mask of Agamemnon is one of the many treasures of the National Archeological Museum.

Rooms 36–39 have a collection of bronzes including votive offerings found at the Idaean Cave in Crete—mythical birthplace of the god Zeus. Rooms 40 and 41 display artifacts from Egypt covering every era of history in the land of the Pharaohs, including the Ptolemaic period when Ptolemy (a general under Alexander the Great, and therefore of Greek descent) took control of Egypt. One of his descendants was Cleopatra, perhaps this most famous ancient queen.

Second floor room 48 is devoted to finds from Akrotiri, a 16th century B.C. settlement on Santorini in the Aegean. The frescoes found while excavating the site are particularly fine and offer a glimpse into a world lost through a devastating earthquake around 1500 B.C. The remaining rooms on the second floor—49–56—feature an amazing collection of pottery and miniature objects, in contrast to the epically proportioned artifacts on the ground floor.

When you have finished your tour, head one block north to Pedion Areos, a large park area created in the 1930s, where you can enjoy the fresh air before continuing your explorations.

From Omonia to Syntagma

Three major thoroughfares run parallel between Omonia Square and nearby Syntagma Square. Stadhiou is perhaps the busiest, with several major department stores and high-class stores that sell jewelry and the best designer names, plus two modern stoas packed with bookstores. When you reach the small square of Klathmonos you'll find the **Museum of the City of Athens** housed in the former King Otto's palace of the 19th century. Nearer to Syntagma, in Koloktroni Square, is the **National Historical Museum** with a collection of artifacts dating from post-Classical times. This is a useful museum to visit if you have a particular interest in post-independence Greece, as many artifacts add detail to the individuals and incidents that shaped the new country.

Northeast of Stadhiou is Panepistimiou (University Street), officially named Elefthería Venizélou after the Cretan statesman. This also plays host to several important buildings. **The National Library**, **University**, and **National Academy** all sit here, confirming it as the academic and intellectual heart of modern Athens. All three are

Neo-Classical in design and made of Pentelic marble, helping to give a feel of how the Agora of the ancient city may have looked at its prime. The Academy (1859) is perhaps the most impressive of the three and was designed by Theophilus Hansen—pre-eminent architect of his generation. A native of Denmark, Hansen was responsible for the Zappion and Royal Observatory in Athens, and numerous buildings in Vienna, Austria. The seated figures of Plato and Socrates sit guarding the Academy entrance and an intricately carved pediment depicts the gods and goddesses of the ancient world; these were sculpted by Leonídas Drósis. Come and look at these carvings through binoculars to get a feel of how richly decorated the temples and communal buildings of the ancient world originally were. Walking towards Syntagma you'll pass the Renaissance-style **house of Heinrich Schliemann**, that most famous of archaeologists, who was instrumental in turning the myth of the Mycenaeans and the Trojan War into fact.

The outward-most thoroughfare is Akadimias, which runs behind the Library, University, and Academy. Opposite these buildings you'll find the Athens Cultural Center housed in a former hospital dating from the 1830s. There are auditoria and cultural exhibitions here, and a small Theater Museum has displays charting the development of this art since ancient times.

Syntagma Square—officially Plateia Syntagmatos or Constitution Square—is perhaps the "emotional" home of modern Athens. It is dominated by the imposing façade of the **Parliament building** or Vouli, which was built as the new royal palace following independence, officially opened in 1836. The use of Pentelic marble on the façade with a Doric-style prolylaia above street level echoes use and form in the ancient city. In front of the building, the

The Memorial of the Unknown Soldier was built to honor all Greeks that were lost to the travesty of war.

Memorial of the Unknown Soldier commemorates all Greeks who have fallen in war. Decorated with a modern carved relief of a Classical theme, the marble is inscribed with the words of an oration by Pericles to honor the dead of the wars of the Peloponnese—it is said that the tombs of these ancient soldiers lie under this very spot. The tomb is guarded day and night by the **Évzones**—traditionally dressed soldiers who became Royal Guards, and then presidential guards following the war of independence. The formal "changing of the guard" takes place every Sunday at 10:45am, however the members of the Évzones have a duty switch every hour during the day when two new guards take the place of the old. This is one activity that you shouldn't miss on your trip to Athens.

The **Grande Bretagne Hotel** on a nearby corner of the square was built in 1842 and has become an Athens institution during its lifetime. During WWII it became military headquarters of both the Germans and the British. Winston Churchill survived a bomb attack here during his stay in December 1944.

Surrounding Syntagma

Numerous major thoroughfares converge on Syntagma, so it's always busy with traffic. The new Metro station also brings a steady stream of people. Still there is shade and a flower garden in the middle of the square where locals and visitors alike rendezvous for lunch or dinner dates.

Behind the Parliament building are the verdant landscaped grounds of the **National Gardens**. These were formerly for exclusive use of the Royal Palace but now form an oasis within the city with formal gardens, water features, and a children's playground. In the south of the garden you will find the **Zappion Hall**, an imposing Neo-Classical building designed by Hansen as a National Exhibition Center in 1888. It now houses a modern conference center.

A five-minute stroll from Syntagma down Avenue Amalias (or through the National Gardens) brings you to another ancient site. At the confluence of Avenues Amalias, Syngrou, and Vas. Olgas is **Hadrian's Gate** built as a triumphal arch in A.D. 131 to mark the divide between the ancient city and his "new Athens." To the east of the gate is the Olympieion, site of the largest temple ever built on Greek soil.

The **Temple of Olympian Zeus** is dedicated to Zeus, "king" of the Greek gods. It was imperative that his temple should be fitting for his position, and its dimensions—250 m (814 ft) long and 130 m (426 ft) wide, with columns of over 17 m (61 ft) in height—are truly majestic. The temple took 700 years to complete and it was Hadrian who finished the task in the second century A.D. One hundred and eight columns originally surrounded an inner sanctum that protected a gold-and-ivory statue of Zeus. Today only 15 are still standing, but their Corinthian capitals have a wonderful form and elegance. In ancient times, the temple sat close to the banks of the River Ilissos creating an even more beautiful vista. Today the river still flows, but its path lies beneath the city.

Nearby, along Vas. Olgas, is the impressive **Olympic Stadium**, sitting in the lea of Ardittou Hill. The stadium was constructed for the ancient Panathanaic Games when each of the surrounding city-states sent delegations to compete. During Roman times beast-baiting also took place here. Dating from the third century B.C., the complex was refurbished for the games of A.D. 144 but was disused and left to decay after the fall of the empire. When the modern Olympic Games were convened in 1896, the stadium was refurbished as the flagship arena, and today it stands as a symbol of the global athletic movement. Witness the heroic statues that stand in the entranceway. Athens will once again host the games in 2004, but the central athletic complex will be at Kifissia—a northern suburb linked to the downtown area by bus and Metro.

Leading directly east from Syntagma Square is Avenue Vas. Sofias. This main thoroughfare, with a number of major embassies, leads to several important museums all within strolling distance or close to the Evangelismos Metro station. Closest to Syntagma is the **Benáki Museum**, a collection donated to the state by Andónis Benáki on his death in

1954. Benáki was born in a Greek community in Egypt, and many of the artifacts on display originate from this other ancient land, though there is a good range of Classical and Roman statuary, and collections from the Early Christian and Byzantine eras including two paintings by El Greco.

On the same side of the street walking away from Syntagma is the **Museum of Cycladic and Ancient Art** run under the auspices of the Goulandrís Foundation. This museum celebrates the art dating from before the development of Athens citystate—discovered in the Cyclades islands of the

Hadrian's Gate was built in A.D. 131 to separate the old city from the "new" Athens.

Aegean (c2000–3000 B.C.) A wonderful collection of naïve figurines carved in marble was discovered in graves on the islands. Most of the figures are female, suggesting the worship of fertility or an earth-mother religion. Maps and drawings help visitors better understand this mysterious ancient people. In addition, the museum shows around 300 objects dating from Classical, Hellenic, and Roman Greece including a collection of finely preserved bronze vessels. One wing of the museum is housed in a beautiful Neo-Classical house designed by Bavarian architect Ernst Ziller for Othon and Athina Stathatos, a prominent Athenian couple. This has

*When exploring the archaeological sites of Athens and the
surrounding area, Lycabettus is of great importance.*

been painstakingly restored and presents a beautiful streetside façade.

Across Avenue Vas. Sofias you'll find the **Byzantine
Museum** housed in a splendid 19th-century mansion built
for Sophie de Marbois, wife of one of Napoleon's generals.
She was a stalwart of Greek nationalism. The museum holds
a wealth of artifacts from the early Christian and Byzantine
eras, concentrating on the religious themes that were so
important in unifying the Greek world at this time. The collection was amassed from churches all across Greece and
Asia Minor (on the western coast of modern-day Turkey).
On the ground floor, the interiors of several churches of dif-
fering ages have been reassembled to explain the develop-

ment of architectural styles — very useful if you intend to visit a range of churches during your stay. The upper floors display excellent examples of icons and frescoes, vestments, and other religious objects.

Immediately next door to the Byzantine Museum is the **War Museum**, a modern building constructed during the military dictatorship. Outside you'll see a range of fighter jets, and missiles, while the galleries inside display historic uniforms, armor, and hand-held weapons. Upper floors concentrate on military tactics and battle plans, examining campaigns from ancient times to WWII.

Behind Evangelismos Metro statio, and next door to the Hilton Hotel is the **National Gallery**. The original compilation was boosted in the 1880s by a large bequest by art collector Aléxandros Soútzos, but the two collections were only brought together in this gallery in 1976. Much of the permanent collection comprises 19th- and 20th-century Greek art and post-Byzantine icons, though you can also find works by El Greco, Picasso, and Delacroix.

From the National Gallery it is just a short walk past the Hilton Hotel along Vas. Sofias to the **Megaron**, a vast new national auditorium and concert hall now holding regular theatrical and musical performances. Look for a dramatic modern sculpture in glass depicting a human figure running at an extremely high speed (or blown by the wind) that graces the main intersection here.

Lycabettus and Kolonaki

To the west of the bare sheer rock of the Acropolis is a rival hill — the verdant pine-clad **Lycabettus**, which makes an inviting diversion from the archaeological sites of the city. Here you'll be able to sit in shade and listen to the birds. The hill was never settled in ancient times because there was no water supply. You can reach the upper slopes by funicular. When you reach the top station, walk to the small chapels of **Ayios Isidoros** and **Ayios Georgios**—center of the Easter celebrations for the city —a modern amphitheater for summer performances, and wonderful views across Athens where major attractions are pointed out on marble panoramas. Though there are fixed telescopes here, having your own binoculars is a boon to really take in the detail.

Surrounding the lower slopes of Lycabettus on the south and west sides is **Kolonaki**, perhaps the most fashionable district of central Athens. Apartments and houses here are much sought after as they sit among chic boutiques, designer stores, restaurants, and bars. It is one of the best parts of the city to eat out in the evening with a range of good international eateries in addition to traditional Greek tavernas.

EXCURSIONS

There's no doubt that Athens is a fascinating city, but with the rush of traffic and the push of the crowds, even these attractions can begin to pall after a few days. Luckily you are perfectly placed to take in numerous excursions for the day or a few days—either on an organized itinerary or under your own steam. This city break can truly be a "three- or four-in-one" vacation if you wish.

Piraeus

Situated only 10 km (6 miles) south of Athens, and almost indistinguishable from the sprawling capital, is Piraeus. This city of over half a million people is actually the third largest Metropolis in Greece, and is its largest port. Although many people simply use Piraeus as a departure point for the myriad Greek islands of the Aegean, the city has its own attractions, being settled since ancient times.

This was not the port that served the city-state of Athens because it could not be seen from the city and was therefore vulnerable to attack. It was first settled around 500 B.C.

> **Carry binoculars to allow for close inspection of the ancient remains.**

when long defensive walls were built from Athens to the sea. By the time of Philip of Macedon it had become a thriving commercial port. Though it fell into decline, as did Athens, through the late first and second millennium, it was re-energized following independence. Its location so close to the new capital ensured its commercial success. Today Piraeus is, above all, a working city with some less than prosperous areas. Stay on the main thoroughfares as you explore.

Taking the Metro (the overland electric railway section) from downtown Athens costs only 250drs and brings you directly to the waterside. Huge quaysides in the Main Harbor cater to hundreds of ferries large and small, and you'll see fleets of large container ships laying anchor offshore. Walking south along the quaysides brings you to a small shady square with the **Cathedral of Agia Triada** on its northern flank. Take this street (Dimokratias) to the Town Hall and visit the lively daily market that takes place in the surrounding streets.

Take a right down Lampraki to reach the pretty **harbor of Zea**. This is one of the marinas used for pleasure craft, and where Athenians—rich and not so rich—moor their boats. These range from simple rowing boats of just a few feet in length to hundred-foot ocean-going vessels. A wide promenade —Akti Moutsopoulou—frames the bay and this is where local people come to stroll in the evenings and on weekends— you can sit at a portside café and watch the world go by.

North from Zea harbor is another pretty harbor, **Mikrolimani** (Small Harbor) or **Tourkolimani**, where you'll find the fishing fleet and some good fish tavernas. Or head south towards the main historical attractions of Piraeus.

From the south side of Zea harbor it is only a short walk to the **Archaeological Museum of Piraeus**. The rather dour building hides a treasure-trove of statuary and other artifacts found during excavation of the ancient shrines of the city, and communal buildings such as the Agora. Pride of place goes to the Piraeus Kouros, the oldest full-size bronze figure depicting the god Apollo. On the grounds of the museum are scant remains of the ancient Theater of Zea.

Walking further south along the promenade past remnants of the ancient sea wall brings you to another small bay where you will find the **Hellenic Maritime Museum**, a semicircular museum with small garden in front complete with cannon. Rooms display an eclectic series of artifacts with dioramas of the great Battle of Salamis in 480 B.C., letters from the naval

Fishing boats float blissfully along the harbor of Poros Town as the sun sets.

heroes of Greek independence, and numerous items salvaged from the seas around the Attica coastline.

The Saronic Islands

The islands closest to Athens are those of the Saronic Gulf, the nearest only 40 minutes from Piraeus by hydrofoil. These represent a total contrast to the bustle of the city and a perfect antidote to the acres of concrete you find there.

Hydrofoils for the Saronic islands depart from Quay I at Piraeus Harbor.

Aegina

This is the closest island to the mainland and the pretty quayside of Aegina Town, with its Neo-Classical buildings, awaits as you disembark. You'll see a pretty whitewashed church protecting the harbor entrance. Stroll along the water's edge past the colorful fishing fleet, have lunch at a seafront taverna, or buy some of the pistachio nuts or local ceramics for which the island is famed. The resort of Agia Marina is 15 km (9 miles) from the town on the west coast and has a good child-friendly beach, and most people make a trip to the nearby fifth century B.C. Temple of Aphaia for some more history.

Aegina is a delight out of season, but can be very busy, especially on summer weekends. Many houses on the island are second homes for wealthy Athenian families.

Poros

Poros lies less than 152 m (500 ft) from the Greek mainland, off the northeastern coast of the Argolid Peninsula and 55 minutes from Piraeus by hydrofoil. Small sailboats crowd the narrow straits and it's a yachtsman's paradise in the summer months. Poros Town—the only settlement on the island

— is a maze of narrow winding streets rising up a small hill. The seafront is the hub of all activity with tavernas and cafés lining the waterside. The rest of Poros is covered with verdant pine forest and the coastline is dotted with small rocky coves — great for swimming and snorkeling.

A 5-km (3-mile) hike to the interior brings you to the remains of the Temple of Poseidon where the famous Greek orator Demosthenes committed suicide in 322 B.C. rather than surrendering to Alexander the Great's forces.

Hydra

Only 1 hour 15 minutes from Athens by hydrofoil, Hydra is the most exclusive of the Saronic islands, and your approach into the harbor is the most dramatic. The beautiful port of Hydra Town keeps its secret hidden until the very last moment and when the panorama comes into view it's time to get the camera ready. Above the shoreline of the narrow cove lie a series of low hills, and each of these are blanketed with Neo-Classical Italianate mansions painted in myriad dusty hues. There are no cars on Hydra—only donkeys. No sandy beaches make the water some of the clearest in the area for snorkeling.

Still, most people don't visit Hydra for any activity other than to "see and be seen." In the 1960s the island was an artist colony and today it has developed into a place for the beautiful people. The boutiques are some of the most exclusive in the Mediterranean, intermingled with the Bohemian craft galleries, exclusive restaurants, tavernas, chic cafés, and Greek ouzeries.

If you don't want to "max" your credit card, don't worry —Hydra has not yet lost its charm that is free-of-charge. You can simply enjoy strolling along the narrow streets with a pretty view on each corner before you head back to Athens on the late hydrofoil.

Spetses

At two hours away from Piraeus by hydrofoil, Spetses is the most remote of the Saronic islands and less crowded with Athenians than the three other islands. There are some good sandy bays to enjoy, and Spetses Town—sleepy by day yet with a vibrant nightlife—offers a good mooring spot for sailboats. Perhaps a little too far for a day trip, Spetses could make a good option for a two-part vacation.

Corinth and the Argolid

The history of Ancient Greece is littered with the feats of city-states led by great leaders, of which Athens is of course the most famed. Within a day's journey of the capital are the sites of two such city-states in an area known as the Argolid. These can be viewed as part of an action-packed day (either independently or as part of an organized tour) but make an excellent two- or three-day excursion for those who want to take it at a more gentle pace.

Corinth

In ancient times Corinth rivaled Athens in its power and influence. It mimicked the layout of the larger city—a town radiated out from the base of a rocky pinnacle that housed religious temples—though at Corinth the hill is much higher than at Athens.

The site was first settled by Mycenaeans because it had an excellent natural water supply, and it reached its first level of prosperity around the seventh century B.C. It became Athens' enemy when it sided with the Spartans during the devastating wars of the fourth century B.C. but the city recovered quickly from the defeat and had a second period of influence that began during the third century B.C. when Philip of Macedonia made it the capital of

In the 1890s, the opening of the Corinth Canal eased local shipping efforts.

the Corinthian League. In 195 B.C. it became head of a group of independent Greek cities of the Achaean League. Ravaged by the Romans in 170 B.C. it rose again from the ashes and was a bustling city when St. Paul came to preach here. He won more support than in Athens and planted the seeds of a very successful early Christian church. Several major earthquakes in the early Christian era saw the city's final decline.

Luckily for us the modern city of Corinth lies several kilometers to the northeast of the site and this leaves much of the ancient city for us to explore. Most prominent as you approach the site is the **Temple of Apollo** built in the sixth century B.C. and one of the oldest buildings in Corinth. Many other remains date from the Roman era, including ornate entrances round the **Fountain of Peirene** where you can still hear the waters flowing through caves at the rear, and the **Lechaion Road** that linked the city to Athens—with worn cart tracks clearly visible in the marble slabs. The site museum has some interesting finds and has a number of dioramas depicting Corinth as it would once have looked.

After visiting the ancient city head up the hill to take in the magnificent site of **Acrocorinth** standing sentinel above. Fortified since the seventh century B.C. the summit is criss-crossed with miles of high stone walls dating from this time that were expanded during the Byzantine and Ottoman eras. At the summit, within three layers of protective wall, are the remains of a Temple of Aphrodite, an early Christian Basilica, Byzantine cisterns, a Frankish Tower, and Ottoman mosques and fountains — this is Greek history in a nutshell!

Though the modern city of Corinth has little to draw the visitor, a modern engineering marvel lies just outside its boundary. The **Corinth Canal** cuts the narrow isthmus that links the Peloponnese with the Greek mainland and splits the Saronic Gulf from the Gulf of Corinth (this links to the Adriatic further west). Sailing around the Peloponnese to Athens not only added extra time to the journey, but also carried ships through some of the most dangerous waters in the Mediterranean — especially in the winter. Ancient Greeks did not attempt to sail around but portaged their huge vessels across the 6 km (4 mile) wide isthmus, and as early as A.D. 67, the Roman Emperor Nero was making the first attempts at cutting a canal. It would not become reality for another 1,825 years. In 1893 after eleven years of digging, a channel 70 m (328 ft) deep, 25 m (85 ft) wide with 8 m (26 ft) of water opened for shipping, taking a single ship at a time between the two gulfs.

The Argolid

From the 15th to the 11th century B.C., this rocky peninsula was one of the most important centers in the known world.

It was from here that the mighty Mycenaean empire grew to encompass mainland Greece and the northern Aegean islands. The exploits of the Mycenaeans, and their greatest leader Agamemnon, were thought to be myth, until the archaeologist Heinrich Schliemann set out to find evidence of the sites of Homer's stories of Troy and Mycenae. He was successful in doing both, and transformed the world of archaeology—and man's view of history.

Schliemann found the remains of the city of **Mycenae** buried under thousands of years worth of debris in a sheltered valley some 60 km (40 miles) south of Corinth. It was so well hidden that the site had been completely forgotten, and it surprisingly had not been plundered by robbers. The military might of the Mycenaeans had been well documented by Homer, but nothing could prepare the archaeologists for the artistic treasures found at the site. As they dug through the remains, the tombs of several kings were discovered; each skeleton lay where it had been carefully buried, the faces covered in a mask of pure gold. Exquisite statuary and intricate jewelry found in the family tombs below show a softer side of these enigmatic people and brought the world of Agamemnon to life. All the artifacts from the site were taken to Athens and many are now on display in the National Archaeological Museum.

The archaeological site of Mycenae, now stripped of its treasures, still makes a majestic scene though it is rather smaller than one might imagine. The large **Cyclopean Walls** —huge rough-hewn blocks of granite laid one atop another with extreme precision—are so called because their enemies could not believe that humans could be responsible for the construction and gave the credit to the one-eyed giant of myth. These date from around 1250 B.C. and surround and protect the inner sanctum through which the only entrance is

The hidden entrance to the Beehive tomb, a favorite destination of touring schoolchildren.

the world-famous **Lion's Gate** decorated with the earliest known monumental sculpture in Europe.

Immediately as you enter the compound you can get a bird's-eye view of **Grave Circle A**, where the Royal grave shafts were found, and then climb to the top of the settlement to view the remains of the **Royal Palace**. From here the views of the surrounding rolling countryside are magnificent.

Half a mile below the city is an immense **Beehive tomb** cut into the hillside and lined with stone blocks. The

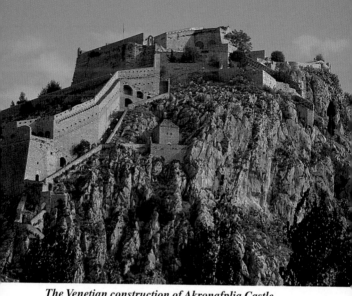

*The Venetian construction of Akronafplia Castle
is a must-see when visiting the town of Nafplio.*

acoustics inside the tomb are very precise, exaggerating the
sound of your approaching fellow visitors. If a party of
schoolchildren arrive to test out the tomb, it may be a good
idea to beat a hasty retreat for the sake of your ears!

Further east from Mycenae is another ancient site also
renowned for its acoustics. The **Theater of Epidauros**
(Epidavros), was built in the fourth century B.C. and could
hold an audience of 12,000 people. Live performances still
take place here every summer. The theater does not sit in

---

splendid isolation but was part of a large settlement based around the **Sanctuary of Asklepios**—one of the most important centers of healing in the ancient world. Today there is little left of the site and it is difficult to imagine hospitals, spas, and faith-healing practices catering to travelers from across the Greek world.

The port town of **Nafplio** makes the perfect base for touring the area, or perhaps a spot to have lunch while on your tour. Set on the south coast of the Argolid, it has been a strategic strongpoint for centuries and boasts no less than four castles dating from Byzantine and Venetian times— on far more ancient foundations—called **Akronafplia Castle**. The modern settlement has an urbane gentility with an old-town of grand Italianate mansions linked by cobbled walkways. Pretty tavernas set tables out in the street and tempt you with fresh seafood caught by the small fishing boats in the harbor. The seaside promenade flanked by smart cafés is where you'll find locals and Athenians alike strolling in the cooling evening air. Look out towards the tiny fortified island of **Bourzi**; you can even take a boat trip to explore the castle if time allows.

Sounion

The windswept peninsula of southern Attica reaches out towards the Aegean Sea, and at its very tip (70 km/43 miles south of Athens) the ancients built a beautiful **Temple to Poseidon**, the God of that watery realm. The views from here are beautiful whatever the time of day—but the sunsets are particularly spectacular.

The temple itself is one of the finest in Greece. Of the 34 Doric columns only 15 are still in situ, and the ornate frieze on the pediment and entablature has been ravaged by the salty air, but the whole effect of the building combined with the setting—with beach on one side and sheer drop on the other—is magnificent.

Sounion is reached by following the coast road from the capital down through several lovely resorts with private beaches. Glyfáda is the closest to Athens and Vouliagméni is the furthest away.

Daphni and Eleusis

Athens has a beautiful downtown area but it is one of the largest cities in Europe, and it also has an industrial element mostly based around the southern and eastern suburbs. Incongruous among the landscapes of oil refineries and factories you'll find historical gems to explore. Ten kilometers (6 miles) west of Athens is the **Monastery of Daphni** (soon to be linked with the downtown area by Metro extension) built on the site of an earlier Temple of Apollo. Founded in the fifth or sixth century A.D., the site was refurbished and extended in the 11th century but sacked and abandoned before being occupied by Orthodox monks in the 16th century. Restoration took place after WWII and again in the 1960s. The pretty Byzantine church (c1080) has a stone-and-tile dome exterior but is famed throughout Greece for the fantastic mosaics that decorate the interior, particularly that of Christ Pantocrator in the main dome.

Through this same industrial area runs the Sacred Way that linked Athens with the city of **Eleusis**. In ancient times the way was lined with shrines and tombs, which are now and again brought to light when redevelopment takes place. Eleusis was home to the Sanctuary of Demeter and the Eleusian Mysteries —a series of complex and enigmatic rituals only performed by initiates of the order. The order thrived from the Mycenaean era to the coming of Christianity. Annual celebrations to Demeter took place in Athens each September, with a public

festival and a secret religious rite that transformed chosen fol-
lowers into initiates of the secrets. A procession would leave
Eleusis and walk along the Sacred Way entering Athens via the
Sacred Gate at Kerameikos (see page 49) before proceeding to
the Acropolis.

In Eleusis the sacred way led directly to the Sanctuary of
Demeter and a large **Temple of Artemis** with a forecourt
where the initiates would gather in preparation for the procession. A great **Propylaia** marked the entrance to the town
—a copy of that at the Acropolis. The **Precinct of Demeter**
lay in a walled complex, and its inner sanctum, the **Periklean
Telesterion**, where only initiates were allowed to enter, sat
within the temple. You will also find the remains of more
mundane structures such as the **Bouleuterion** and **gymnasium**. A museum on site displays extremely good artifacts
found among the ruins.

Delphi

Where the mysteries of Eleusis were only open to a few initiates, advice from the Oracle at Delphi was open to all. It
was simply a matter of making your way to the Sanctuary of
Apollo, now three hours by road from Athens to the northwest. In ancient times this was the spiritual center of the
Greek world and people would travel by land or sea to consult the gods. No important decisions of state could be made
without consulting the Oracle here, and when the Colossus
of Rhodes was toppled in an earthquake the people of that
city-state in the Aegean left it where it lay after advice from
the Oracle not to rebuild it.

There has been a temple here since pre-historic times
when Gaia the Earth-Mother goddess was worshipped. Even
in these early times the gods would be consulted with the
oracle issuing their verdicts from the Rock of Sybil. Later,

HIGHLIGHTS

The Acropolis and Acropolis Museum. On the Acropolis; Tel. (01) 3214172. Religious center of ancient Greece with the remains of many important temples. Open Mon 11am–6:30pm, Tues–Sun 8:30am–6:30pm. Admission fee.

Sanctuary of Dionysus. Odós Thrasylou; Tel. (01) 3224625. Site of the main ancient Greek Theater. Open daily 8:30am–2:45pm. Admission fee.

The Plaka District. Athens Old Town dating back to the Ottoman and Byzantine eras. The pretty traffic-free streets are a delight to explore.

Museum of Greek Folk Art. Odós Kidathineon; Tel. (01) 3213018. Collection of Greek embroidery, woodwork, and ceramics. Open Tues–Sun 10am–2pm. Admission fee.

The Roman Agora. Odós Pelopida; Tel. (01) 3245220. Center of daily life during the Roman era. Open Tues–Sun 10am–2pm. Admission fee.

The Greek Agora. Odós Adrianou 24; Tel. (01) 3210185. Birthplace of democracy and social heart of ancient Athens, with the remains of many important political and religious buildings. Open Tues–Sun 8:30am–3pm. Admission fee.

Kerameikos. Odós Ermou; Tel. (01) 3463552. A site spanning both sides of the ancient city wall and Sacred Gate. The site includes the main cemetery of the city. Open Tues–Sun 8:30am–3pm. Admission fee.

The National Archaeological Museum. Odós Patission 44; Tel. (01) 8217717. The world's foremost collection of ancient Greek art and statuary. Open Summer (1 Apr–15 Oct) Mon 12:30pm–7pm, Tues–Fri 8am–7pm, Sat–Sun 8:30am–3pm; Winter (16 Oct–31 Mar) Mon 11am–5pm, Tues–Fri 8am–5pm, Sat–Sun 8:30am–3pm. Admission fee.

Byzantine Museum. Vas. Sophias 22; Tel. (01) 7211027. A collection relating to religious structures and artifacts of the early Christian and Byzantine eras. Open Tues–Sun 8:30am–3pm. Admission fee.

Benaki Museum. Odós Koumbari 1; Tel. (01) 3671000. Collections of artifacts dating from prehistoric times to the Ottoman era. Open Mon, Wed, Fri, Sat 9am–5pm, Thurs 9am–midnight, Sun 9am–3pm (closed Tues). Admission fee.

The Museum of Cycladic Art/Goulandris Museum. Neophytou Douka 4; Tel. (01) 7228321. Collection of early art and funerary finds dating from the third millennium B.C. found in the islands of the Cyclades in the Aegean. Open Mon, Wed, Thu, Fri 10am–4pm, Sat 10am–3pm (closed Sun, Tues). Admission fee.

Temple of Olympian Zeus. Vas. Olgas; Tel. (01) 9226330. Remains of the largest temple ever built in ancient Greece to the "king" of the gods. Open daily 8:30am–3pm. Admission fee.

EXCURSION SITES

Delphi. Home of the ancient Oracle of Delphi, where pilgrims could visit to consult with the gods. Open daily 7:30am–6:45pm (museum hours same as site except Mon 11am–6pm). Admission fee.

Corinth. Ancient city that once rivaled Athens in power and influence. Open daily 8am–5pm. Admission fee.

Mycenae. Site of the city of the Mycenaeans and home to King Agamemnon who fought the Spartans at Troy. Open daily 8am–5pm. Admission fee.

Epidauros. The finest ancient theater in the Greek world renowned for its acoustics. Open daily 7:30am–7pm. Admission fee.

Sounion Temple to Poseidon On one of the finest sites in Attica (the area surrounding Athens), overlooking the sea. Open daily 8am–7pm. Admission fee.

The ruined temple of Athena Pronaia can be found at the spiritual site of Delphi.

Olympian gods usurped Gaia but the sanctuary retained its role. Legend says that the God Apollo arrived at Delphi by sea on a dolphin and slayed the monstrous python that guarded the entrance to the sanctuary. Thus the temple was named in his honor.

A modern road cuts through the remains and the approach to the site from the parking lot leads first to the **Roman Agora**, where pilgrims would stock up on supplies and offerings for the temple only a few minutes away. Here you can see the remains of the **Sanctuary of Apollo**, the nearby waters of the **Kastalian Springs** where pilgrims would purify themselves before their consultation, and the **Rock of Sybil** where the oracle proclaimed the verdict of the gods. The modern museum has a wonderful collection of statuary, treasure, and other artifacts found at the site.

Below the road are the remains of a large gymnasium, and the temple of **Athena Pronaia** where pilgrims would make their first religious stop on the climb to the sanctuary. Its *tholos* (columned rotunda) is set in a beautiful wooded lot with the sanctuary on the hillside behind.

WHAT TO DO

ENTERTAINMENT

Athens comes alive after dark with a range of activities to fill your diary. However, you'll probably need to alter your normal routine to enjoy it as the locals do. Theater performances are followed by a late leisurely dinner, often after 11pm, and if you intend to head out to a nightclub, don't expect to start until around midnight.

Even if you only want to sample the delights of Greek tavernas and perhaps stroll around Plaka, the real atmosphere starts after 9pm when Greek families come out to eat. If you can hold your appetite that long you'll have a much more authentic experience.

A nighttime view of the majestic Acropolis explains the popularity of the Sound and Light Show on the hill.

Athenscope is a free publication that lists all activities taking place during the time of your stay, but here are the major forms of entertainment that you could enjoy.

Theater: Ancient Greeks were credited with inventing drama and comedy in the theater, and this tradition carries on into the present. The city boasts around 50 theaters and the season is a popular one lasting from October to May. Most of the performances are in Greek. The Athens Festival runs from May to September with a full program of cultural events ranging from choral concerts to dance to recitals with performances aimed at visitors as well as Athenians. For details of the program contact the Greek National Tourist Board at Odos Voukourestiou 1, Tel. 01-9694500.

The following theaters stage performances for tourists, or performances that would appeal to international audiences. The National Theater and Concert Hall, Tel. 01-7282333, more commonly known as the Megaron, is situated on Vas. Sofias, next to the Megaro Mousikis Metro station. It has a program of new and established works in addition to choral, opera, and other musical performances by Greek and international musicians and dance groups.

The Roman Odeon of Herodes Atticus near the Acropolis holds classical performances on summer evenings. The seating has been renovated so there is no fear of sitting on worn stone, but this is perhaps your greatest opportunity to view a performance as the ancients did. Tel. 01-3232771 for details.

Lycabettus Theater on Mount Lycabettus also holds regular summer performances but is less likely to be internationally oriented. For program details, Tel. 01-7227233.

Sound and Light Show: The history of the Acropolis is brought to life through dancing lights and an informative narration, and the surrounding darkness really allows you to study the beauty of the Parthenon. This is a must for all visitors. Performances take place nightly May to October in English at 9pm. Tel. 01-3225904 for details.

Traditional Music and Dance: Greece has a rich legacy of folk dance and music, though genuine performances are becoming more difficult to find, particularly in the capital. Dora Stratou Folk Dance Theater presents performances of traditional Greek song, dance, and music at a traditional "folk-village"-type auditorium on Philopappos Hill from May to September — daily except Mondays. Tel. 01-3244395 for ticketing details and prices.

INTER-ISLAND CRUISING

Take a trip to one of the islands of the Saronic Gulf where you can enjoy the laid-back atmosphere of the towns, and the fresh air — a total contrast to the bustle and noise of the city. Have a long lunch at one of the many tavernas — the seafood is great! — and do a little shopping before returning to Athens on the late ferry. See excursions in the Where to Go section for some ideas.

SPORTS

The proximity of Athens to the coast offers a great opportunity to combine beach activities with a city vacation. Traveling by taxi from a downtown hotel, it only takes 30 minutes to find some excellent facilities. Much of Athens closes down during the heat of August (though not those relating to tourism) and many people head to the coast for the cooler air, therefore you find the resorts very busy at this time. The season is short, with many hotels opening in May and closing again in September. The closest resort to the city is Glyfáda, only 12 km (7 miles) from the city. Its proximity to Athens makes it extremely busy, especially on weekends and it lies very close to the approach to the old airport, which in the past resulted in a lot of aircraft noise. Twenty kilometers (12 miles) away is Voúla, a little less crowded than Glyfáda. Vouliagméni is 5 km (3 miles) further south, and a haunt for the local Athens jet-set because of the spa situated at the sulphur lake that gives the resort its name. For more details about spa treatments, Tel. 01-8960341. There are a number of luxury hotels situated here. Each of these resorts has a Greek Tourist Board–approved beach with changing facilities, food, and watersports. There is a small entrance fee.

You'll find a full range of sports offered: from tennis, windsurfing, and waterskiing to snorkeling and diving — however it is fair to say that the underwater world so close to the capital can be disappointing.

The Saronic islands have a longer season — stretching from April to October. Aegina and Spetses are particularly well-organized with regard to watersports and beach activities, but if you want to relax on the beach it may be better to spend at least one night on Spetses as it is a two hour boat trip from Piraeus.

For those whose city hotel doesn't have a pool the following two hotels allow non-guests to enjoy the facilities for an admission fee — the Athens Hilton 46, Vas, Sofias Ave, Tel. 01-7720201; and the Caravel Hotel, Vas, Alexandras Ave, Tel. 01-7290731.

Other sports

Sailing: Weekend and summer sailing is very popular with Athenians as the crowded marinas such as those at Pireaus testify. Tournaments occur regularly throughout the summer, and even the children have their own league competitions. Several companies have boats to rent — with crew or "bare" if you have a skipper's certificate. Contact the Hellenic Sailing Federation, Odos Xenofondos 15, Tel. 01-3235560 for more details.

Fishing: You don't need to be a professional angler to enjoy a relaxing day's fishing. Just about every male over the age of five can be found sitting on the sea wall waiting for a bite and it is amazingly relaxing to be letting the rod do all the work. Or you can rent a small boat and head out into deeper water. Contact the Amateur Anglers and Maritime Sports Club at Moutsopoulou Quay, Tel. 01-4515731 for more details.

Golf: There is an 18-hole golf course at Glyfáda, Tel. 01-9846820.

Snow Skiing: The nearest facilities can be found at Mount Parnassus (from December–March), a two-hour drive from the city. The hotels of Delphi and Arachova lie only twenty minutes from the slopes if you want

These children know that simple fishing from the quayside may prove fruitful.

a village atmosphere. Contact the Greek Alpine Club at Arachova, Tel. 01-2324555 for more details.

As in any major city, Athens has sporting facilities in the form of private clubs and community centers. The Olympic Athletic Center of Athens at Odos Kifisias 37, Marousi (Tel. 01-6834060) has a range of excellent facilities including nine swimming pools, basketball courts, and a velodrome — all for use during the 2004 Olympic Games.

Spectator Sports

Football (soccer): Football is a national obsession for the Greeks and Athens' teams (Panathanaikos and AEK Athens) feature prominently in domestic and European competitions. The season runs from September to May. Panathanaikos Football Stadium is located at Kifissia, a northern suburb — this will be the major stadium for the 2004 Olympic Games, which will be held in the city. Ask your hotel if it is possible to get tickets as these are difficult to come by.

Horseracing: Athens Race course can be found at the bottom of Syngrou Avenue where racing takes place on Mondays, Wednesdays, and Saturdays. Plans have been drawn up to redevelop the course as part of the Athens 2004 Olympic program, so make enquiries with your hotel or the EOT before making the journey out to the course.

SHOPPING

Athens offers a multitude of shopping opportunities, not only for typical Greek-style souvenirs, but for haute couture, good art, and jewelry. The good news is, whatever your budget, you're bound to find something exciting to take home — whether you want mass-produced items or unique hand-finished pieces. As with any large city, individual districts specialize in certain types of goods, so here is a short rundown of what is available.

Where to Shop

For undeniably tourist kitsch, head for the streets of Plaka and you'll find mass-produced items of all kinds. They are interspersed with galleries, T-shirt shops, and numerous street hawkers selling fun toys or handmade budget art.

The Monastiráki flea market is a great place to search for unique bargain items.

Monistiráki is the old bazaar area of the city — the Sunday flea market is a must for collectors of old china, memorabilia, and furniture — and the myriad small shops sell all kinds of collectibles in addition to good-value street clothing.

Kolonaki is the favorite district of Athenians for the boutiques and home furnishings stores that sell the best of European design. Prices match the quality here, but if you don't want to spend, just sit at a streetside café and watch the Athens jet-set do a little shopping.

The maze of streets around the Cathedral offers religious souvenirs of all kinds. Incense burners, icons, and tamata — votive offerings — are the most portable.

Athens Municipal Market just south of Omonia Square offers wonderful fresh food for you to enjoy as you stroll, as well as numerous Greek foodstuffs to take home.

The streets of Ermou, Eolou and Stadiou offer large department stores and numerous pan-European names with everything from shoes and clothing to household wares.

In many parts of the city prices are flexible — though not in department stores and boutiques — and haggling is expected at the flea market. In tourist shops, you may get a discount for cash, and prices are lower early and late in the season. Conversely, you may be charged a little extra if you want to pay by credit card.

What to Buy

Copper and brassware: Copper and brass have been used for many household utensils for centuries and skilled craftsmen still work in small workshops around the city. The newly produced goods have a bright patina that mellows with use, and some of the older pieces are exceptionally beautiful. Antiques stores in Monastiráki have the best choice and these include urns for carrying water, samovars, bowls, and tureens. Ornate Ottoman tables on folding wooden bases are compact enough to carry in hand luggage, as are serving ladles and goat bells.

Ceramics: The skills honed at Kerameikós centuries ago are still much in evidence on the streets of Athens. You can buy exquisite hand-thrown and painted copies of ancient pieces for a price, and numerous examples of less expensive factory produced items. Traditional shapes of urns, jugs, and cups are decorated with scenes taken from the lives of the ancients or of the Greek gods in their domain on Mount Olympus. Modern ceramic artists also thrive and there are many small galleries showcasing hand created pieces.

Statuary: If you want a little piece of ancient Greece then you'll certainly be able to find it. It will be a reproduction of course — but still you can own your own copy of Zeus, Poseidon, or Athena herself, small enough to grace a table or large enough to decorate a garden. Plaques depicting ancient friezes, or masks to hang on walls are also extremely popular, as are Mycenaean helmets. If classical statuary is too ornate for your taste, you can also find copies of the minimalist Mycenaean statues found at the Goulandris Museum. The National Archaeological Museum also has a wide range of copies of its artifacts. Each comes with a certificate of authentication.

Leatherware: Local craftsmen have always worked goat and cow hides and the industry continues today. Footwear, bags, and clothing come in a range of styles, though quality is generally more rustic and bohemian than similar items produced in Italy or France.

Carpets and needlepoint: Ottoman craftsmen left behind a legacy in both the use and production of fine carpets — look for hand-knotted ornate patterns in wool or silk which come with a hefty price tag. Hand-produced Greek flotaki rugs were traditionally used in farmhouses across the Greek world and are made from sheep wool. They are sold by weight and are decorated with traditional symbols such as deer, or patterns, such as the Mycenaean geometric designs.

Needlepoint, crochet, and embroidery — once activities undertaken by every Greek woman — are now dying arts, so any hand-crafted pieces will become collectors' items of the future. Machine-produced pieces are readily available in the form of tablecloths, napkins, cushions, and handkerchiefs. Or you could try a traditional embroidered hat complete with long silk tassel, now only worn during folkloric spectacles.

Jewelry: When Schliemann excavated the tombs of the Mycenaean rulers he found their skulls decorated with masks fashioned from pure gold. Since that time Greece has been famed for the worksmanship of this most precious metal and you can still find many high class jewelry stores in Athens producing excellent quality items. Athenians still love to adorn themselves as they did in ancient times with gold, and with precious stones imported from elsewhere. Prices are very competitive as gold is sold by weight with a relatively small mark-up for the craftsman's skill, however always check with prices at home if you intend to make a major purchase. Most popular items are traditional patterns passed down since ancient times. The major museums also sell copies of items displayed, which are quite appropriate souvenirs of your trip.

For those whose taste or budget isn't for precious metals and stones, there is a whole range of jewelry featuring semi-precious stones and street jewelry such as rings, earrings, toe rings, and though not strictly jewelry, worry beads — carried by most Greek men to calm the nerves — are very decorative. The best feature beads of cornelian or amber with silver decoration and silk thread.

Icons and Art: An icon is a religious portrait, usually of a saint or apostle. These were a development from the fayum paintings that covered the face of the dead in the sarcophagi of Egyptian mummies. Icons lie at the heart of Byzantine or Orthodox worship in both the Greek and Russian churches, and they form a focus for prayer — the characteristic gold leaf used in their production symbolized the glory of God.

For centuries they were popular souvenirs of the grand European Tour or religious pilgrimage. However, modern production methods, including thin artificial canvas and gaudy synthetic colors, saw them lose favor.

In recent years there has been a rebirth in icon painting using traditional methods, both for church renovations, and for commercial sale. Natural pigments and egg tempura (egg yolk and vinegar) binding are painstakingly mixed and applied to a canvas bound over wood. The gold leaf is then applied and the whole image is given a patina. This time-consuming work is exquisite and correspondingly expensive. Pre-1821 icons will require an export permit.

You'll find mass-produced icons in many tourist shops, but for quality pieces visit a specialist store.

Icons are a very particular form of art, and if they are

Children will enjoy playing near the duck pond at The National Gardens.

not to your taste there is a whole range of art to choose from. Scenes of Athens and the classical sites are extremely popular as mementos.

Edibles: Wonderful foods from the Greek countryside include honey, olives and olive oil, and nuts such as almonds and hazelnuts. All can be bought in pretty packaging for you to take home. For something a little stronger try ouzo — the aniseed flavor aperitif — or Greek brandy, which is slightly sweeter than French Cognac. Metaxa is the most famous brand name.

THINGS TO DO WITH CHILDREN

Athens requires some forethought if you are taking young children. Not all will be as eager to spend days at the ruins and it can be oppressively hot during the summer months. However, Greeks love children and they will be most welcome and fussed over in tavernas and restaurants, which makes eating out a delight.

Here are some ideas for a child-friendly visit:

Take a boat trip to one of the nearby islands. A Metro ride to the station at Pireaus means you only have to cross a highway to reach the ferry port, and numerous destinations are only an hour or two away. Children will love the journey and the magic of reaching a seaside destination.

Take time out in the cool gardens of the capital. The National Gardens have a lake with water birds and a playground, and Areos Park, near the National Archaeological Museum, has play facilities for children.

Let your children have their portraits done — street artists can be found in Plaka — or their faces painted. Either way they get to be the center of attention.

If all else fails, a day at the beach will surely blow the city cobwebs away. Take a break at Glyfáda, Voúla, or Vouliagméni — only a short taxi ride away.

CALENDAR OF EVENTS

1 January: Called Protochronia but also St. Basil's Day, when sprigs of basil are given as traditional gifts.

6 January: Epiphany — crosses are thrown into harbors on the coastline and islands. The young men who dive and retrieve them are believed to receive good luck for the coming year.

February — Carnival in Athens. Masked bands of revelers take to the streets. Maypole dancing.

26 March: Greek Independence Day, military parades.

Clean Monday: First day of Lent marked by frugal meals and when house-cleaning and laundry are undertaken with enthusiasm.

Easter: Easter is the most important of the Orthodox holidays. Candlelit processions follow a flower-decked bier on Good Friday. On Holy Saturday a sacred flame is passed to each household to light a lamp of faith. On Sunday, lambs are sacrificed and roasted signifying the commencement of another Spring.

23 April: St. George's Day — celebrates the patron saint of Greece.

1 May: May Day, or Protomagía (Festival of Spring) marked by processions and flower festivals.

June–September: The Athens Festival — drama, opera, music, and dance performances around the city. Dafni Wine Festival with dancing and music.

24 June: Birthday of St. John the Baptist — a festival of feasts and bonfires.

15 August: Assumption Day. Processions and festivals at "Panagia" churches across the city.

28 October: National Ochi ("No") Day, commemorating Greek defiance of the Italian invasion of 1940.

December: Caroling in the days before Christmas and on New Year's Eve.

EATING OUT

You'll find that the staples of Greek cuisine have changed little since Plato's day. It has always taken local and seasonal ingredients at the peak of their flavor and freshness, and served either raw, or cooked in the simplest of fashions — on a grill, or slowly in the oven. The people have relied for centuries on staples such as excellent olive oil, fragrant wild herbs, seafood, and lamb or goat meat, along with an abundance of fresh vegetables, fruit, pulses and nuts, washed down with local wine. Today, the traditional Greek diet is considered one of the healthiest in the world and prices in all but the most luxurious establishments are government-controlled offering excellent value to the visitor.

> **Service is relaxed in Greek tavernas — enjoy the occasion.**

You'll find numerous places to eat excellent Greek dishes in all parts of the capital, but Athens has much more to offer as a culinary center. As with many European capitals it has a thriving restaurant industry featuring extremely good cuisine from around the world. Greeks love to eat out, and welcome the opportunity to try excellent new dishes and restaurants, which range from traditional French "haute" to "avant-garde" fusion cuisine.

Some of the best new international restaurants in the city are listed in the recommended section on page 134, but for those who want to discover Greek cuisine, the following information will help you get the most from your menu.

Where to eat

In Greece you'll find a range of eating establishments. Each different type specializes in certain types of dishes, so here is an explanation of the main names that you'll come across on your visit.

The *ouzerie* is a traditional establishment selling not only the fiery but pleasant aniseed flavored alcoholic drink, but also the *mezédes* dishes that accompany it — ouzo is never drunk on an empty stomach. Octopus (or squid) is traditional but it is not compulsory; you will also have a range of hot and cold vegetable and meat dishes to choose from.

The *psistaria* offers food on the go. It serves gyros and souvlaki. These most ancient of fast food make a tasty lunch or snack.

Wine is served in kilo and half kilo rather then carafe or half carafe.

The *taverna* (you'll find it spelled tabepna on many Greek signs because *b* is pronounced *v* and *p* is pronounced *r* in the Greek language) is at the heart of Greek hospitality. These rustic eateries, often family run, offer a range of local dishes and country wine. This is where most Greek families would eat appetizer and entrée courses.

More up-market eateries are known as *restaurante*; these will have fine tableware and offer nouvelle cuisine.

After your savory courses, peruse the amazing choice at the *zacharoplastia* — pastry or sweet shop — or the *galaktopolio*, which specializes in yogurt, cheese, and other dairy dishes.

The *kafenion* is the Greek coffee shop, traditionally the domain of the male, and still so in the countryside and Greek Island villages. Usually very plainly decorated, with a few old tables and chairs outside, it is the focus of heated political debate and serious backgammon games.

When to eat

Most tavernas and restaurantes will be open to serve lunch and dinner. Lunch is taken at around 2:30pm. Traditionally this would be followed by a siesta before work began again at 5:30pm, but this is changing in the capital. Dinner is eaten late — usually around 10pm, though most establishments will serve food as late as 1am. If you want to eat early, most will begin their evening service at around 7pm. You will definitely have your choice of table if you eat before 8pm, but atmosphere is definitely better later in the evening when local people come out to eat.

Be aware that Sunday is traditionally a day of rest for citizens and many eateries outside the main tourist areas are closed.

The Menu

In most traditional restaurants you will be presented with an extensive menu (often in Greek and English), which lists many seasonal dishes. Items currently available will have a price in pencil beside them.

Olives are a staple on Greek menus — they were a favorite food of the gods!

Some of the best and most authentic tavernas will not even have a menu. You simply go into the kitchen or to the grill to see what looks and smells most enticing, then make your choice. This is probably the best way to familiarize yourself with Greek dishes if you are unsure of what to order.

All restaurants will render a cover charge. This includes a serving of bread and usually does not cost more than 200drs per person.

Appetizers

Greece is one country where appetizers can constitute a full meal. *Mezédes* (a selection of small appetizer dishes) shared by the whole table, is a fun and relaxing way to eat — you

> **"Bon appétit"**
> **— kali órexi**

simply have as little or as much as you want and keep ordering until you have had your fill. Tavernas have no qualms about taking orders for "appetizers only" meals.

Most popular mezédes are *tzatziki*, a yogurt dip flavored with garlic, cucumber, and mint; *dolmades*, vine leaves stuffed with rice and vegetables — sometimes meat — which can be served hot (with *avgolemono* sauce made of eggs and lemon) or cold (with yogurt); olives; *tarama*, cod roe paste blended with bread-crumbs, olive oil and lemon juice; *gigantes*, large beans in tomato sauce; *kalamari*, deep-fried squid; *pastourma,* a kind of garlic sausage made with mutton or beef; and *keftedes*, small meatballs flavored with coriander and spices. *Saganaki* is a slice of feta cheese coated in breadcrumbs and then fried, but you can also have feta wrapped in foil with garlic and herbs and cooked in the oven — delicious! Cretan specialities include *tirópitakia* (small pastry packets filled with goat and ewe cheese) and *salingária* (snails).

Greek salad or *horiatika* (literally translated as "village salad") of tomato, cucumber, onion, and olives topped with feta cheese, can be taken as a meal in itself or can accompany any other dish. When adding salad dressing (bottles of olive oil and wine vinegar are found with other condiments on the table) always add vinegar to the salad first followed by oil. This is done to taste so start with a little of each and take it from there.

Soups are a staple of the diet in winter but availability is more limited in summer. Fish soup, *psarósoupa*, is a standard on many seafood restaurant menus along with *kalamariáki* (spicy squid and tomato). *Avgolemono*, chicken broth with egg, lemon, and rice, although delicious is now less common, and *magirítsa* (tripe soup) is served only at Easter time.

Fish

Athens' proximity to the sea means that fresh fish (*psaro*) is readily available and throughout Attica and the Peloponnese you'll find excellent seafood restaurants. The day's catch is displayed on ice outside a taverna and you will be asked to make your choice, which will be weighed before cooking — ask the price if you are on a budget as seafood is always a relatively expensive option by Greek standards, due to over-fishing. If the seafood

> Cheers (when drinking) — *yámas*

is frozen (a common practice in the heat of summer) this will always be stated on the menu. Seafood is usually grilled (broiled) served with fresh lemon but ask if you want it cooked a different way and most tavernas will accommodate you. Most common are *barbounia* (red mullet), *xifias* (swordfish), *glossa* (sole) and *lithrini* (bream). *Marides* (little fish or whitebait) and *sardeles* (sardines) are served crisp fried. Why not try *psaro mezedákia* (mixed fish plate) with a little of everything, or for the ultimate luxury order *astakós* (giant crayfish, also known as the Mediterranean lobster). If you like seafood stewed, try the octopus (*ktapódi*) with white wine, potatoes, and tomatoes; or *garídes* (prawns), served with white wine sauce, or sauce mixed with feta cheese.

Meat

Fast foods to eat on the run include *gyros* (thin slices of meat cut from a spit and served with salad on pita bread), or *souvlaki* (small chunks of meat on a skewer). More formal barbecued dishes may include whole chickens, sides of lamb, or stuffed loin of pork, all cooked to a melting perfection. If you want a basic steak look for *brizole* on the menu.

The superb slow-cooked oven dishes and stews are well worth trying. *Kleftiko* is braised lamb with tomatoes, while *stifado* is braised beef with onions. Out in the Greek countryside you may also find stewed rabbit, venison, and wild boar on menus during the season.

Greece's most famous dish is probably *moussaka* — successive layers of eggplant and minced lamb with onions topped with a generous layer of béchamel sauce. At its best it should be firm but succulent, and aromatic with herbs. The best restaurants will make a fresh batch daily. *Pastitsio* is another layered dish, this time of pasta (macaroni), meat, and tomato sauce. *Gouvetsi* is beef stewed with small lozenge-shaped pasta.

For those who want a hot meatless dish, *yemitsa* are tomatoes, eggplant, or bell peppers stuffed with a delicious rice and vegetable mixture; or try *horta*, oven-cooked vegetables in a tomato sauce.

Dessert

Most tavernas will bring a plate of seasonal fresh fruit as a finale to your meal. If you feel the need for something more substantial, then a taverna will rarely have a full selection of desserts. The *zacharoplastia* is the place to go. Here, perhaps, is the longest lasting legacy of the

It is easy to find a quick meal for a good price when strolling around Athens.

Turks who introduced a number of incredibly decadent sweets. You will find *baklava*, layers of honey-soaked flaky pastry with walnuts; *katiafi*, shredded wheat filled with chopped almonds and honey; *loukoum* a honey-flavored fritter; or *pitta me meli*, honey cake. If you prefer dairy desserts, try delicious yogurt with local honey or fruit. *Rizogalo* is a kind of cold rice pudding, or try *galaktobouriki*, custard pie.

Café society has made its mark in Athens, transforming the *zacharoplastia* into a coffee or tea shop more easily recognizable to visitors.

Cheeses

Most Greek cheese is made from ewe or goat's milk. The best-known soft cheese is *féta*, popping up in every Greek salad or served alone. *Kaserí*, a hard cheese, is best eaten fresh, but can also be used grated, like Parmesan, and in cooked dishes.

Drinks

Dionysus held sway over legendary Greek wine production that was exported throughout the ancient world. Mainland production in Macedonia, the Peloponnese, and on the islands of Crete, Rhodes, and Santorini have been celebrated throughout history and only lost favor internationally during the Ottoman era when little attention was paid to the vineyards. However, during the latter part of the 20th century modern techniques were introduced which have improved the quality of bottled wines. Names to look for include Boutári and Náoussa.

Many tavernas offer good house wine from the barrel. This basic "village" wine — red/white/rosé — will be served young and cool and it compliments the olive oil base of the cooked dishes perfectly. Enjoy its earthy qualities for a very reasonable price.

Greece also produces a wine flavored with resin called *retsína* — particularly useful in ancient times to keep the wine fresh in the hot climate. It too goes well with the Greek diet, but it is an acquired taste.

Ouzo is taken as an aperitif — neat, or with ice and water — the distilled alcohol flavored with aniseed seems to cool the blood. However, don't overdo it, as too much can pack a mighty hangover!

> **An *ouzo* or *raki* "on the house" to finish a meal is a widespread custom.**

Those who prefer beer can find Amstel and Heineken brewed under license on the Greek mainland, but Mythos is a native Hellenic beer that has a very crisp taste.

Greece produces its own after dinner drinks. Native brandy is sweeter than French Cognac and Metaxa is the best-known brand name. Sold in 3-star, 5-star and 7-star varieties, it is the 7-star which is the most refined.

Non-alcoholic drinks

Greece has fallen in love with the café frappe — strong cold coffee served over ice, which is especially refreshing in the heat of the day. Hot coffee is made *ellenikos* or Greek style (indistinguishable from Turkish coffee), freshly brewed in individual copper pots and served in small cups. It will automatically arrive *glykivastro* (very sweet) unless you order *metrio* (medium) or *sketo* (without sugar), but don't drink to the bottom as it has a generous layer of grounds! Italian espresso and cappuccino can be found in most cafés. Those who prefer instant coffee can order a drink known simply by its trade name — nescafé or nes.

Soda comes in all the international varieties. Enjoy Greek mineral water still or sparkling — Aoli is the most popular brand name.

Reading the Menu

I'd like a/an/some...	**Tha íthela...**
Could we have a table?	**Tha boroúsame na échoume éna trapézi?**
napkin	**trapezo-mandíllo**
cutlery	**machero-pírouna**
glass	**potíri**
one	**ena/mia**
two	**dhío**
three	**tris/tría**
four	**tésera**
bread	**psomí**
wine	**krasí**
beer	**bíra**
fish	**psarí**
fruit	**froúta**
meat	**kréas**
milk	**gála**
sugar	**záchari**
salt	**aláti**
pepper	**pipéri**
honey	**méli**
water	**neró**
egg	**avgó**
beef	**vodinó**
pork	**kirinó**
chicken	**kotópoulo**
prawns	**garída**
octopus	**ktapódi**
eggplant (aubergine)	**melitsána**
garlic	**skórdo**
ice cream	**pagotó**
olives	**elyés**
lamb	**arní**
roasted or grilled	**psitó**
butter	**vútiro**
chick peas	**revíthya**

HANDY TRAVEL TIPS

An A–Z Summary of Practical Information

A

ACCOMMODATIONS

Hotels: Hotels are divided into six classes—Luxury, A, B, C, D, and E. Room rates for all categories other than luxury are set by the Greek government. The classes are dictated by the facilities at the hotel, not by the quality of the rooms. This means that a class-C hotel room may be just as comfortable as a class-A hotel room, but will not have facilities such as a conference room or hairdresser. Most hotels in class C and above are clean and reasonably furnished. The D and E category hotels will have no public rooms and no restaurant.

There are a range of accommodations at each price and quality level in the city but the number of visitors does put pressure on capacity, especially at peak times between May and September. It may be difficult to find the style of accommodations that you want so always make a firm booking before you arrive to avoid disappointment. Between October and April, it may be possible to get a good deal as the city quiets down.

If you travel in peak season there may be a surcharge if you wish to book for less than three days. Local and national tax (around 4% and 8% respectively, plus a service charge of around 12%) will be added to the posted price.

Rooms: Rooms can be rented in family homes in the suburbs of Athens. Always find out about transport connections to the tourist attractions before making a firm booking. Some rooms are evaluated and approved by the EOT. Private rooms will always be clean though simply furnished and prices will be negotiable outside the main season.

If you need advice, the Greek National Tourist Office (GNTO), signposted EOT in Greece, can help with bookings and reservations. They issue pamphlets listing all hotels in each area or island group which are class-C or above.

I'd like a single/double room.   **Tha íthela éna monó/
diplό domátio.**

| with bath/shower | **me bánio/dous** |
| What's the rate per night? | **Piá íne i timí giá mía níkta?** |

AIRPORT

A new international airport called Athens Airport Eleftherios Venizelos is due to open in summer 2001. It lies 15 km (9 miles) southwest of the city at Plata, with rail and road links to the capital.

Flights may still arrive at the old international airport (10 km/6 miles southeast of the city) where non-Olympic Airways international services use the East Terminal. For information, Tel. (01) 9694111. All airline domestic flights use the west terminal (called Olympic Airport); for information, Tel. (01) 9269111. A third terminal caters to all charter flights, Tel. (01) 9972686.

All terminals are connected by shuttle bus services that cost 250drs. Taxis are available at both main terminals. City center transfers cost around 2,500drs. Buses from Syntagma Square connect with all three terminals regularly 24 hours a day; prices vary between 120drs and 500drs, and are more expensive after midnight. Line 91 leaves from the East and Charter Terminals; Line B2 from the West terminal. Line 93 links all three terminals with the port at Pireaus for onward journey to the Saronic and Aegean islands.

B

BUDGETING for YOUR TRIP

Scheduled flight from London prices from £180.

Scheduled flight from New York from $500.

Hotel room in mid-range hotel in high season: 25,000–35,000drs.

Meal in mid-range taverna with house wine (per person): 5,000–7,000drs.

Car rental one day for a small car (*ceicento/atoz*) in high season for one week: 131,000drs unlimited mileage. Prices vary enormously from high to low season.

Taxi fares: old airport into the downtown area 2,500drs.

Metro tickets: 150drs for a two-zone journey on a single line; 250drs per single journey with line transfer; 1,000drs for a 24-hour ticket.
Museum and archaeological site entrance fees: 500–1,500drs.
Sound and Light Show: 1,500drs.
Beach entrance fee at some spots along the coast: 600drs.
One-way ferry ticket to Aegina: 920drs; to Poros: 1,650drs; to Spetses: 2,500drs.
One-way hydrofoil ticket to Aegina: 1,700drs; to Poros: 3,250drs; to Spetses: 5,000drs.

CAMPING

There are no campsites serving the city itself, but the surrounding Attica peninsula, Argolid region of the Peleponnese, and the islands do have facilities that operate in summer. Contact the EOT for details—they issue a pamphlet listing all approved campsites including facilities available at each.

May we camp here?   **Boroúme na kataskinósoume dó?**

We have a tent.   **Échoume mía skiní.**

CAR RENTAL

Athens is a very congested city and the main tourist attractions are centered in such a small area that it makes little sense to rent a vehicle. Using the Metro system will limit the amount of walking you do and taxis are plentiful and cheap. If you want to visit some of the islands it is easier to take the Metro to Pireaus, which terminates just across the street from the main harbor area. However, if you intend to spend a few days touring the Argolid, a car would be an asset.

You will find all the major rental companies either at the airport or with offices in central Athens. Your hotel should also be able to arrange car rental for you.

Hertz: web site <www.hertz.com>; Athens office Syngrou 12, Tel. 9220102; West Airport, Tel. 9813701; East Airport, Tel. 9613652.

Athens

Avis: web site <www.avis.com>; Athens office Amalias 48, Tel. 3224951; West Airport, Tel. 9814404; East Airport, Tel. 9953440.

Budget Car Rental: web site <www.drivebudget.com>; Athens office Syngrou 8, Tel. 9214771; West Airport, Tel: 9883792; East Airport, Tel: 9613634.

Those who want to rent should carry an international driver's license, although a national driver's license is usually accepted, provided that it has been held for one full year and the driver is over 21 years of age. Deposits are usually waived for those paying by credit card.

Insurance is often included in the rental rates but do enquire and read the contract thoroughly to be sure. Collision damage waiver is advisable and if your credit card or home insurance does not provide it, it should be purchased as part of the rental agreement.

I'd like to rent a car (tomorrow). **Tha íthela na nikiáso éna aftokínito (ávrio).**

for one day/a week **giá mía iméra/mía evdomáda**

CLIMATE

Athens has a surprising range of climatic conditions and temperatures throughout the year. August is stiflingly hot and dry with air condition made worse by vehicle pollution, which sits in the valleys. Many Athenians leave the city at this time and it's advisable that you don't visit if you can avoid it. From June until the end of September, the weather is hot during the day and warm in the evenings with 12 hours of sunshine per day. If you travel after September the weather is changeable with rain and windy weather interspersed with more pleasant warm days. Snow can occasionally fall in winter but rain is more common.

	J	F	M	A	M	J	J	A	S	O	N	D
Air Temp.												
Max °C	12	12	16	19	25	32	44	38	29	23	20	15
Max °F	54	54	60	66	76	90	110	100	85	74	65	58

| Min °C | 2 | 7 | 8 | 11 | 16 | 19 | 23 | 23 | 19 | 16 | 11 | 8 |
| Min °F | 35 | 44 | 46 | 52 | 60 | 66 | 72 | 72 | 66 | 60 | 52 | 46 |

Water Temp. (Piraeus)

| °C | 14 | 14 | 13 | 15 | 18 | 22 | 25 | 25 | 24 | 22 | 18 | 16 |
| °F | 57 | 57 | 55 | 59 | 64 | 72 | 77 | 77 | 75 | 72 | 64 | 61 |

CLOTHING

From June to September light summer clothing will be all you need
—with perhaps a wrap for later in the evening. Natural fibers are
most comfortable, especially in the heat of midsummer. Even though
you are in the city it is important to take precautions with your skin
and always carry something to cover arms and legs to avoid sunburn.
Hats and sunglasses are a must in summer.

In spring and fall, take extra layers in case of a cold spell. In winter, bring a heavy coat or rainproof jacket as the city can be cold and
wet. You can still have very pleasant days even late or early in the
year, so a layering system is probably the most practical so that you
can add or take off layers as needed.

If you intend to enter any of the churches in the city you must be
suitably dressed. No shorts for either sex, and women must have
shoulders covered.

It cannot be stressed enough that comfortable, practical footwear
is needed when touring the archaeological sites. Marble steps and
walkways are worn smooth with age and are very slippery; many
surfaces are uneven which can result in twisted ankles.

If you intend to head out to the theater or a fine restaurant, then
take a dressier ensemble with you—Athenians enjoy dressing up,
though for most tavernas casual dress is quite acceptable.

COMPLAINTS

If you have a complaint you should first take it up with the manage-
ment of the establishment concerned. If you get no satisfaction then
you can approach the Tourist Police whose officers are specifically
trained to deal with visitors who have problems. They can be con-
tacted by calling Tel. 171. Officers will speak English.

Athens

CRIME and SAFETY

Central Athens is generally a safe place to visit with no inherent threats to visitors; however, just as in many large cities petty crime can be a problem (pick-pocketing and theft from vehicles) so it pays to take some basic precautions.

Never carry large amounts of cash.

Leave all valuables in the hotel safe.

Always walk in well-lit streets at night.

Do not leave valuables visible in vehicles.

Always use official taxis—yellow ones.

It is always useful to have copies of important paperwork such as ticket numbers, passport number, travelers' check numbers just in case you do find yourself the victim of crime.

CUSTOMS and ENTRY REQUIREMENTS

EU citizens can enter Greece for an unlimited length of time. British citizens must have a valid passport. Citizens of Ireland can enter with a valid identity card or passport.

Citizens of the US, Canada, Australia, and New Zealand can stay for up to three months on production of a valid passport. South African citizens can stay for up to two months on production of a valid passport. No visas are needed for these stays. If you wish to extend these time-scales you must obtain a permit from the Aliens Bureau, 173 Alexandras Avenue, 11 522 Athens, Tel. (01) 770 5711.

Visitors may import and export up to 10,000 Greek drachmas. There are no restrictions on travelers' checks, however sums of over $1,000 or its equivalent in cash must be declared on entry.

Greece has some strict regulations about the import of drugs. All the obvious ones are illegal but also some seemingly beneficial drugs such as codeine or tranquilizers are also banned. Medicines prescribed by a doctor for personal use are permitted so if you take any drug on medical advice always carry enough for your needs and keep it in its original container.

The Greek authorities are very concerned about the loss of antiquities and national treasures. If you intend to buy an old piece, be it an icon or some statuary, always deal with a reputable dealer and keep your receipts. Genuine antiquities will need a permit. Exporting antiquities without a permit is a serious offense.

For citizens of non-EU countries, allowances for goods bought duty-free to be carried into Greece are as follows;

200 cigarettes or 50 cigars or 250 grams of tobacco.

1 liter of spirits or 4 liters of wine.

250 ml of cologne or 50 ml of perfume.

DRIVING

Road conditions: Roads in the city are always crowded with traffic and you can usually make better progress walking than driving. Drivers jostle for position, often running a changing light, and drivers seem to park wherever they please. Always keep a look out all around you if you are driving or walking.

In order to cut traffic pollution, the Greek government has introduced various measures including only allowing local vehicles with odd-numbered license plates to use the roads on odd-numbered days, and even-numbered cars on even days—weekdays only. This includes rented vehicles with local Athens license plates.

Out in the countryside the roads have no verges/shoulders, only dust and stones at the side of the macadam. This can cause problems if you need to slow and leave the highway. If you get caught in a summer storm the road surface can become very slippery.

Rules and regulations: Greece drives on the right and passes on the left, usually yielding to vehicles from the right—though this is not always followed by drivers. Most road signs are international and easily understood, however one problem in navigating can be a lack of names in the Latin script under the Greek lettering. Since many place names in Roman lettering are spelled phonetically, you may find the same village name is spelled several different ways as you drive along.

Athens

Speed limit on open roads is 100 kmh (65 mph) and in towns 50 kph (30 mph) unless otherwise stated, although many local people and visitors do not adhere to the regulations. Both speed limit and distance signs are in kilometers.

Seat belts are compulsory, as are crash helmets when riding a motorcycle. Drunk driving laws are strict and road patrols can test you and issue on the spot fines.

Many districts have one-way systems to ease the flow of traffic around the narrow streets. Be aware that many moped riders (and some car drivers) do not obey these rules.

Fuel costs: Fuel is extremely cheap by European standards at around 300drs per liter. Gas stations are open every day in season, between the hours of 9am and 7pm.

If you need help: If you have an accident or breakdown while on the highway put a red warning triangle some distance down the road to warn oncoming traffic.

Always carry the telephone number of your rental office when you travel. They will be able to advise you if you have difficulties. In case of accident or theft, contact the Tourist Police, Tel. 171, who will send an English-speaking officer to help you. The Greek motoring organization ELPA provides roadside assistance. If you are a member of an affiliated assocation in your own country you will be able to get help without charge (check this before you depart), otherwise they will make a charge. Contact number in case of difficulty is Tel: 104.

Road signs: Most road signs are the standard pictographs used throughout Europe. However, you may also meet some of these written signs:

ΑΔΙΕΞΟΔΟΣ	No through road
ΑΛΤ	Stop
ΑΝΩΜΑΛΙΑ ΟΔΟΣΤΡΩΜΑΤΟΣ	Bad road surface
ΑΠΑΓΟΡΕΥΕΤΑΙ Η ΑΝΑΜΟΝΗ	No waiting
ΑΠΑΓΟΡΕΥΕΤΑΙ Η ΕΙΣΟΔΟΣ	No entry

ΑΠΑΓΟΡΕΥΕΤΑΙ Η ΣΤΑΘΜΕΥΣΙΣ	No parking
ΔΙΑΒΑΣΙΣ ΠΕΖΩΝ	Pedestrian crossing
ΕΛΑΤΤΩΣΑΤΕ ΤΑΧΥΤΗΤΑΝ	Reduce speed
ΕΠΙΚΙΝΔΥΝΗ ΚΑΤΗΦΟΔΙΑ	Dangerous incline
ΕΡΓΑ ΕΠΙ ΤΗΣ ΟΔΟΥ	Construction in progress
ΚΙΝΔΥΝΟΣ	Caution
ΜΟΝΟΔΡΟΜΟΣ	One-way traffic
ΠΑΡΑΚΑΜΠΤΗΡΙΟΓ	Diversion (detour)
ΠΟΡΕΙΑ ΥΠΟΧΡΕΩΤΙΚΗ ΔΕΞΙΑ	Keep right

Are we on the right road for ...?	**Imaste sto sostó drómo giá ...?**
Full tank, please.	**Na to gemísete me venzíni.**
Check the oil/tires/battery.	**Na elénxete ta ládia/ta lásticha/ti bataría.**
My car has broken down.	**Épatha mía vlávi.**
There's been an accident.	**Égine éna distéichima.**

 E

ELECTRICITY

The electric current in Greece and the islands is 220 volts/50 cycles. Electric plugs are of the European continental two/three prong type. Adapter plugs are available from electrical stores but it's better to buy at home to be sure.

an adapter/a battery   **énas metaschimatistís/ mía bataria**

EMBASSIES and CONSULATES

Australian Embassy and Consulate
37, D. Soutsou Street, 115 21 Athens,
Tel. (01) 645 0404; fax (01) 646 6595.

British Embassy and Consulate
1, Ploutarchou Street, 106 75 Athens,
Tel. (01) 723 6211; fax (01) 724 1872.

Athens

Canadian Embassy
4, Gennadiou Street, 115-21 Athens,
Tel. (01) 727 3400; fax (01) 727 3460.

Irish Embassy
7, Vass. Konstantinou Avenue, 106 74 Athens,
Tel. (01) 723 2771/2; fax (01) 724 0217.

New Zealand General Consulate
268 Kifissias Avenue, 15323 Halandri, Athens,
Tel. (01) 687 4700; fax (01) 687 4444.

South African Embassy and Consulate
60, Kifissias Avenue, 151 25 Maroussi,
Tel. (01) 680 6645; fax (01) 680 6640.

US Embassy and Consulate
91, Vass. Sophias Avenue, 115 27 Athens,
Tel. (01) 721 2951; fax (01) 645 6282.

EMERGENCIES

Police main number	Tel. **7705711**
Police emergency	Tel. **100**
Tourist Police	Tel. **171**
Fire	Tel. **199**
Ambulance	Tel. **166**
Duty Pharmacy	Tel. **107**

G

GAY and LESBIAN TRAVELERS
Greece is traditionally a very conservative country where traditional family relationships form the backbone of society. However, there is a natural courtesy towards visitors and this combined with the number of different types of international tourists makes Athens a good destination for gay and lesbian travelers.

GETTING THERE

Olympic Airways (web site <www.olympic-airways.gr>) is the national carrier of Greece. It operates international flights to Athens from the following destinations: New York, Toronto, Melbourne, London, and Manchester. It operates to and from the following European cities for flight connections from the UK, US, Australia, New Zealand, and South Africa: Amsterdam, Brussels, Frankfurt, Geneva, Zurich, Milan, Rome, and Paris.

Numerous other international carriers fly into Athens. These include Lufthansa (web site <www.lufthansa.com>), KLM (web site <www.klm.com>), Swiss Air (web site <www.swissair.com>) and British Airways (web site <www.britishairways.com>). Connections from the US to Europe can be achieved with American Airlines (web site <www.aa.com>), Delta Airlines (web site </www.delta.com>), Continental Airlines (web site <www.continental.com>), Virgin Atlantic Airlines (web site <www.virgin-atlantic.com>). From Australia and New Zealand you can reach Europe for continuing flights to Greece with Singapore Airlines (web site <www.singa-poreair.com>), Thai Airways (web site <www.thaiair.com>), Qantas (web site <www.qantas.com>) and Air New Zealand (web site <www.airnewzealand.co.nz>).

By Car: The overland route to Greece from western Europe has long been a problem because of difficulties with the former Yugoslavian countries. However you can drive to the Italian ports of Ancona or Brindisi and take an overnight ferry to Patras on the Greek mainland. It is then a two-hour drive to Athens. For details of services and prices contact Superfast Ferries (Hellas), Amalias 30, 10558 Athens; Tel. (01) 3313252; fax (01) 3310369; web site <www.superfast.com>.

By rail: The route is again problematic because of the disrupted route through the former Yugoslavia. Rail services from western European capitals can link with the ferries at Ancona or Brindisi for onward sailing to Patras and rail transfer to Athens. For those who wish to visit Athens as part of a European train "tour" there are special prices for monthly passes and special ticket prices for those under 26 and over 65. Contact <www.eurorail.com> or the Rail Europe Travel Centre, 179 Piccadilly, London W1V 0BA; Tel. 0990 848 848 for information and reservations.

GUIDES and TOURS
Only Greek Tourist Board-approved guides are allowed to conduct tours of archaeological sites. You will find official guides at the entrance to the Acropolis, or you can book a personal guide through any EOT office.

There is a great deal of choice if you want to book a guided tour of Athens. These can constitute a morning, full day, or an evening and include transport to and from your hotel. A hotel concierge will be able to organize this for you, or the EOT will have details of approved companies.

H

HEALTH and MEDICAL CARE
Emergency treatment is given free but this covers only immediate treatment. EU residents (including UK and Irish nationals) will be able to get further free treatment but must carry a form E111 to obtain it. E111 forms must be validated before you leave. This is done at any main post office.

It is always advisable to take out health/accident insurance to cover you for a health emergency while on a trip. Insurance will reimburse the cost of protracted treatment or repatriation should the need arise.

There are no vaccination requirements for your trip to Athens. The tap water is safe to drink but doesn't taste very good. Bottled spring water is universally available.

As mentioned in the Customs section above, many medicines and prescription drugs obtained normally in other countries are banned in Greece. If you are taking any medication always take enough for your needs while on your trip and always keep it in its original packaging with original labels in case the customs agents have a query about it.

If you have a basic medical need look for a pharmacy, or pharmakio, signified by a green cross, where you will be able to obtain basic advice. Most pharmacists will speak some English. Telephone 173 to obtain more information about pharmacists.

If you visit Athens in the summer, always protect skin against sunburn and keep yourself well hydrated.

If you have a health emergency, dial 106 for an ambulance or to find the nearest open hospital.

HITCHHIKING

Hitchhiking is not illegal in Greece, however city public transport is comprehensive and inexpensive, which means that few travelers hitchhike as a method of getting around. It is more common to hitchhike in the countryside but this is a dangerous method of travel even in relatively safe destinations such as Greece. Women traveling alone are especially at risk.

HOLIDAYS

National Holidays fall on the following dates.

1 January:	New Years Day or Protochroniá.
6 January:	Epiphany.
25th March:	Greek Independence Day.
1 May:	May Day.
15 August:	Assumption of the Virgin.
28 October:	National "No" or "Ochi" Day.
25 December:	Christmas Day.
26 December:	St. Stephens Day.

Moveable dates center around the Easter celebrations with the first day of Lent (Clean Monday), Good Friday, Easter Monday, the Ascension, and Holy Monday (Whit Monday). They change with each calendar year.

LANGUAGE

The Greek language of Homer and the ancients is no longer used in day-to-day affairs, which means that there are in fact two Greek languages: *katharévousa* which is the language of the elite, the courts, and of the ancient texts, and *dimotikí* which is the language written and spoken by most Greeks today.

The Greek alphabet differs from the Roman in that the pronunciation of some individual letters covers two distinct letters in the Roman alphabet. This is the reason for so many spellings of the same place name on road signs around the island—for example, the word *ágios* is often also spelled *ághios* and *áyios* in the Roman alphabet, though the pronunciation is the same.

In the center of Athens you'll find most street signs, and lots of tourist information (including taverna menus) printed in English, but here is a run-down of the Greek alphabet to help you get started with pronunciation.

Α	α	a	as in bar
Β	β	v	
Γ	γ	g	as in go*
Δ	δ	d	like th in this
Ε	ε	e	as in get
Ζ	ζ	z	
Η	η	i	like ee in meet
Θ	θ	th	as in thin
Ι	ι	i	like ee in meet
Κ	κ	k	
Λ	λ	l	
Μ	μ	m	
Ν	ν	n	
Ξ	ξ	x	like ks in thanks
Ο	ο	o	as in got
Π	π	p	
Ρ	ρ	r	

Σ	σ, ς	s	as in kiss
T	τ	t	
Y	υ	i	like **ee** in m**ee**t
Φ	φ	f	
X	χ	ch	as in Scottish lo**ch**
Ψ	ψ	ps	as in ti**ps**y
<u>O</u>/ Ω	ω	o	as in g**o**t
<u>OY</u>	ου	oo	as in s**ou**p

Don't worry if you don't speak any Greek. You will find that most people working within the tourist industry will have a basic English vocabulary and many speak English very well. Your will also find that the *Berlitz Greek Phrase Book and Dictionary* and *CD Pack* cover nearly all the situations you're likely to encounter in your travels.

LAUNDRY and DRY CLEANING
Major hotels will offer laundry and dry cleaning services but will charge a premium for the service.

When will it be ready?   **Póte tha íne étimo?**

M

MAPS
The Greek Tourist Office produces an excellent street map to aid your exploration of the downtown area and Pireaus. It includes all the main public transport routes. You can also use the *Pocket Map to Athens* issued by the Ministry of Transport and Communications, which has more detailed information about transport, including prices and timetables.

MEDIA
Television: Most large hotels will offer satellite TV stations including CNN and BBC News 24.

Radio: Athens municipal radio 98.4FM has news broadcasts in English Mon–Fri at 8:30am and 4:30pm. BBC World Service can be found on 107.1FM.

Athens

Press: Numerous English-language newspapers (US and UK) are available at hotels and newsstands in the city. Some may be one day old. The Paris-based International Herald Tribune is published daily and is available on the day of printing. Athens Today is a daily newspaper published in English. It reflects Greek news items and domestic concerns in addition to features and commentary on international issues. Athenscope is produced weekly in English and covers all cultural events happening in the week ahead. You can also find items of interest in Athens Today and This Week in Athens — though their listings are more limited. You'll find them in hotel lobbies or tourist offices.

MONEY

Currency: Until January 2002 the currency is the Greek drachma, abbreviated to drs and it is found in coins of 5, 10, 20, 50, and 100drs, and notes of 50, 100, 500, 1,000, 5,000, and 10,000drs. From that date, Greece will adopt the Euro as its national currency, which will consist of notes of 5, 10, 20, 50, 100, 200, 100, and 500 euros; each euro comprises 100 cents and coins will be issued in denominations of 1, 2, 5, 10, 20, 50 cents and 1 and 2 euros.

There is no limit to the amount of foreign currency you may import to Greece. You may import 100,000drs and export 20,000drs. Have an official Greek exchange receipt to show the teller if you want to change your drachmas back into your domestic currency before returning home.

Currency Exchange: Most banks will operate currency exchange for foreign currency and travelers' checks and will charge a percentage commission for the service; this varies but is usually between 1% and 3%. Exchange rates should be published on a notice board inside the bank or in the window and are generally the same for each bank. Main Post Offices will also operate currency exchange services with an 800drs fee for amounts up to 100,000drs.

You can also exchange money and travelers' checks at commercial exchange centers found in all the tourist centers. These are often open longer hours than the banks. Some of these advertise commission-free transactions but exchange rates vary so you will need to decide which give the better deal.

You will always need to prove your identity when exchanging money, so take your passport with you.

Automatic Teller Machines (ATMs): National Bank of Greece and Ionian Bank operate ATMs which accept Cirrus and Plus cards. Other banks will also provide the facility—look for the Cirrus or Plus logo above the machine. Many banks have ATMs that will dispense cash against major credit cards. Again, look for the card logo above the machine.

Electronic Currency Exchange: Next to an ATM you may also find a currency exchange machine, which will accept notes of all major currencies and deliver you Greek drachmas/Euros in exchange. Just follow the instructions (in English and other languages) carefully.

Credit Cards: Many hotels, restaurants, ticket offices, and shops accept credit cards, but there is still a minority who do not. Some companies may charge extra for credit card payments, to cover their extra costs. It is always advisable to ask about credit card acceptance before you sign the register or order your food, to avoid difficulties later.

I want to change some pounds/dollars.	**Thélo na alláxo merikés líres/meriká dollária.**
Do you accept traveler's cheques?	**Pérnete "traveler's cheques"?**
Can I pay with this credit card?	**Boró na pliróso me aftí ti pistotikí kárta?**

OPEN HOURS

Banks are open Mon–Thurs 8am–2pm, Fri 8am–1:30pm.
Shopping hours vary considerably. Most shops open Mon–Fri 9am–1:30pm, 5:30–8:30 and Sat 9am–3pm, however tourist shops

—in Plaka for instance—will open seven days a week from 9am–10:30pm.

Museums and archaeological sites are generally open Tues–Sat 9am–5pm, Sun 9am–3pm, but there are exceptions to the rule.

The main Post Office is open Mon–Fri 7:30am–8pm; Sat 7:30am–2pm; Sun 9am–1:30pm.

P

POLICE

The Athens municipal police force wears greenish-grey uniforms in summer, green uniforms in winter. Tel. 100 for emergencies or Tel. 770 5711 at other times.

Tourist Police (Tel. 171)—these officers will speak English.

POST OFFICES

Post offices, painted bright yellow with the initials EΔTA, are generally open from 7:30am–2pm. Stamps can be bought here and at kiosks and tobacconists/newsstands for a small premium. Mailboxes are also painted yellow but may be red in post offices. Packages for non-EC countries should not be sealed until they have been checked by post office staff. Post offices also handle exchange, check cashing, and money orders.

The main post office in Athens can be found at 100 Odos Eolou (near Omonia Square), Tel. 335 3356. Opening hours Mon–Fri 7:30am–8pm; Sat 7:30am–2pm; Sun 9am–1:30pm.

Price for sending a postcard: to other EU countries—180drs.

for other destinations—200drs.

PUBLIC TRANSPORTATION

Metro: The Athens underground and surface urban railway — the Metro — offers an efficient and cheap service. Trains run every 4 minutes during rush hour and every 6–10 minutes at non-peak times between the hours of 5am and midnight. Three lines link the downtown area to Pireaus and Dafni in the south; Kifissia and Ethniki

Amyna in the north. The system was expanded and city center stations upgraded in the late 1990s.

Tickets cost 150 drachmas for one journey with 2 zones with no transfer, 250 drs for one journey with line transfer, and are valid for 60 minutes from the time of validation — machines validate each ticket as you enter the station area. You can buy tickets valid for 24 hours at a cost of 1,000drs.

When's the next train to…?	**Póte févgi to epómeno tréno giá…?**
single (one-way)	**apló**
return (round-trip)	**me epistrofí**

Buses: There is an extensive bus network running many places that the Metro doesn't reach and they run from 5am–11:30pm. However the buses can be crowded with local Athenians coming and going, especially at peak times and for short journeys it may be more comfortable to walk or get a taxi. Ticket prices are 120drs per journey, but books of 10 tickets are also available. Augmenting the bus system are electric trolley buses operating on set routes, with the same price structure.

As a general guide, bus numbers beginning with 0 operate in central Athens; those beginning with 1 operate in the southern coastal suburbs as far as Vougliameni; 2 to the south central suburbs; 3 and 4 to southeastern and central Attica; 5 to Kifissia and the northern suburbs; 6 and 7 to the northwest; 8 westwards towards Dafni; 9 towards Piraeus.

The Athens Transport Office (OASA) issues a free map showing Metro line routes and the routes of the buses in the downtown area. This can be obtained from Tourist Offices and from the OASA office at Odós Metsóvou 15. This is located one street north of the National Archaeological Museum.

Taxis: Taxis are numerous and cheap (they are painted yellow and have the sign TAXI atop the vehicle and on the side) but although they should have meters which they set at the start of each journey, most don't work and so its best to agree on a price for your journey before you get into the car. Officially, government set prices are as follows: 200drs minimum fare; 66drs per kilometer within the city; 50 drs per suitcase in the trunk. As a guide you should pay 2,500drs from the old airport to the city. Prices are posted at the taxi stand at the airport. In the city you can hail taxis in the street but extra long or short distances may be unpopular with drivers. All hotels will call a taxi for you that will pick you up at the reception.

Ferries: The ferry system is inexpensive and reliable though ticket prices may rise as new craft augment the aging fleet. Daily services operate to all the nearby islands from Piraeus to the south of Athens for the islands of the Saronic Gulf, and Rafina to the Sporades islands to the northeast. For details of all services, contact Pireaus Port Authority, Tel. (01) 451 1310; Rafina Port Authority, Tel. (0294) 22300; Saronicos Ferries, Tel. (01) 412 6181 (operates services to all the Saronic Gulf islands).

The fastest services are offered by the "flying dolphin" services. These hydrofoils can carry over 200 people and cut the journey time to the Saronic islands by at least 50% over regular ferries (you'll reach Aegina in around 40 minutes). The main companies are Ceres Ferries and Flying Dolphins, Tel. (01) 4280001; Minoan Flying Dolphins, Tel. (01) 4199000.

R

RELIGION

The national religion of Greece is the Greek Orthodox Church. Other religions that have representation in the city include:

Church of England—St. Paul's, Odos Philellinon 29.
American church—St. Andrew's, Sina 66.
Roman Catholic—St. Denis, Panepistimiou 24.

T

TELEPHONE

The Telecommunications Company of Greece or OTE (known to everyone as oh-tay) controls domestic and international communications in Greece. Most public telephones now accept cards for both international and domestic calls rather than coins. Purchase cards at OTE offices in 100 unit, 500 unit, and 1,000 unit capacities. Kiosks and newsstands also sell the smaller unit cards. OTE offices have call booths where you can make international calls and pay after you have finished your call. The main OTE office in Athens is at 15 Stadiou Street, Tel. (01) 3215899. The office is open Mon-Fri 7am-midnight, weekends and holidays 8am-midnight. There is also an office at 85 Patission Street that is open 24 hours a day.

Most hotels of C class and above have direct dial international lines but add a huge surcharge to the cost of your call. Avoid this by using your credit card and direct call center, or a pre-pay international card with an access number. Many American service providers have international access numbers offering quick and easy connection. Make enquiries before you leave home.

The international code for Greece is 30.

The area code for Athens is 01 followed by a 7-digit number. If calling from outside Greece drop the 0 from the code.

International country codes are as follows, all prefixed by 00.

Australia	**61**
Canada	**1**
Ireland	**353**
New Zealand	**64**
South Africa	**27**
United Kingdom	**44**
United States	**1**

Athens

TICKETS

There is no central ticketing organization in the city. Each venue must be approached separately.

TIME ZONES

Greece operates two hours ahead of Greenwich Mean Time and also operates summer time—moving the clocks one hour forward during the summer.

New York	London	Dublin	Jo'burg	**Athens**	Sydney	Auckland
5am	10am	10am	11am	**noon**	7pm	9pm

TIPPING

Service is included in restaurant and bar bills although it is customary to leave any small change on the table. If you have a young boy or girl bring you water or clear your table it is customary to give them a few coins.

Taxi drivers expect a 10% tip.

Unless service is included (do check as many will add 12% to the price of the room), hotel chambermaids should be left a tip of around 300drs per day. Bellhops and doormen should be tipped up to 500drs, depending on services provided.

Attendants in restrooms should be left around 100drs.

TOILETS/RESTROOMS

All the main tourist attractions have good public facilities. Metro stations should also have them, as will communal parks. Most cafés will have facilities—these vary in cleanliness—but you should be a patron of the café to use them, so do order a drink or snack.

TOURIST INFORMATION

Two organizations are responsible for producing and dispersing tourist information about Greece. The Greek National Tourist Organization (GNTO) works on external promotion. They have a network of offices throughout the world. For Tourist Information before you travel to Greece, contact one of the following offices.

Australia and New Zealand

Greek National Tourist Organization
51-75 Pitt Street
Sydney, New South Wales.
Postal Address is P.O. Box R203 Royal Exchange,
New South Wales 2000, Australia.
Tel. (2) 92411663-5
fax 92352174

Canada

Greek National Tourist Organization
1300 Bay Street, Main Level
Toronto, Ontario M5R 3K8.
Tel. (416) 968-2220
fax (416) 968-6533

There is also an information office at 1170 Place du Frère André,
Suite 300, Montreal, Quebec H3B 3C6. Tel. (514) 871-1535; fax
(514) 871-1498.

United Kingdom and Ireland

Greek National Tourist Organization
4, Conduit Street
London W1R 0DJ.
Tel. (020) 7434-5997
fax (020) 7287-1369
e-mail <eot-greektouristoffice@btinternet.com>.

United States of America

Greek National Tourism Organization
Olympic Tower, 645 Fifth Avenue
New York, NY 10022.
Tel. (212) 421-5777
fax (212) 826-6940
e-mail <gnto@greektourism.com>.

Athens

Greek National Tourism Organization
168 North Michigan Avenue, Suite 600
Chicago, IL 60601
Tel. (312) 782-1084
fax (312) 782-1091

Greek National Tourism Organization
611 West Sixth Street, Suite 2198
Los Angeles, CA 92668
Tel. (213) 626-6696
fax (213) 489-9744

Ellinikos Organismos Tourismu (EOT) handles tourist information within Greece. For tourist information while in Athens, official EOT offices can be found at the following address.

Head Office
2, Amerikis Street
P.O. Box 1017
105 64 Athens.
Tel. (01) 322 3111; fax (01) 322 4184

WEB SITES
Web sites for useful organizations have been included in other sections of this guide, however, the following web sites will help you to plan your trip to Athens:

<www.gradus.com>
<www.greekembassy.org>
<www.athensguide.com>
<www.accessathens.com>
<www.vacation.net.gr>

WEIGHTS and MEASURES
Greece uses the metric system for weights and measures.

Length

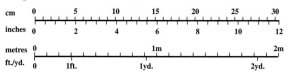

Weight

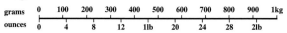

Temperature

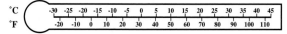

Fluid measures

Distance

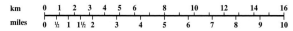

YOUTH HOSTELS

For details of youth hostels in the city contact the national Youth Hosteling Organization in your own country or the Greek Youth Hostel Association, Odós Dragatsianou 4, Athens; Tel. (01) 323 4107.

Recommended Hotels

Hotels in Greece are rated by the Greek Tourist Organization (OTE) according to facilities available. The highest is De Luxe moving down the scale to Luxe, A, B, C, D, and E. All hotels will be clean; those in C class and above will be reasonably furnished. All hotels in the higher grades must have restaurant and conference facilities, but standard and comfort of rooms may not be higher than those of a lower class hotel.

Athens has a good range of hotels in all price categories. It is a year-round tourist city but the peak season is from June to September when pressure is put on the total number of tourist beds available. Always make a firm booking at all standards of hotel if you are visiting at this time. Prices rise and fall with the seasons — with a difference of as much as 40% between high and low season. Do check whether tax and service charges are included in the price as this can add up to 17% on to prices. The same applies to a charge for breakfast.

The following recommendations cover all of the main central districts of Athens and offer hotels for all budgets. To make a telephone enquiry or booking, the numbers below have the regional code included. Always preface the number with the international code 00 30, and drop the first 0 from the district code if you are calling from outside Greece.

Prices indicated below are for a double room in high season.

$ 20,000 drs and under.
$$ 20–35,000drs.
$$$ 35–50,000drs.
$$$$ 50–65,000drs.
$$$$$ over 65,000drs.

ACROPOLIS AND MAKRIYIANNI

Divani Palace Acropolis \$\$\$\$\$ Odós Parthenonos 19-25, 117 42 Athens; Tel. (01) 928 0100; fax (01) 921 4993; web site <www.otenet.ge/divaniacropolis>. A large hotel situated close to the Acropolis (to the south), the Divani Palace offers a good standard of accommodations and caters to individual travelers and tour groups. Rooms have A/C, satellite TV, phone, dataport, mini-bar, hairdryer. Facilities include 24-hour room service, small pool, roof garden with view of the Acropolis. The basement floor features preserved remains of an ancient city wall. 253 rooms. Major credit cards.

Philippos \$\$–\$\$\$ Odós Mitseon 3; Tel. (01) 922 3611; fax (01) 922 3615. Set in the shadow of the Acropolis (to the south), this small hotel makes a good base for the archaeological sites and the pleasures of the Plaka area. Rooms have A/C, TV, phone. Facilities include restaurant, bar, parking. 48 rooms. Major credit cards.

KOLONAKI

St. George Lycabettus \$\$\$\$–\$\$\$\$\$ Odós Kleomenous 2; Tel. (01) 729 0711; fax (01) 724 7610; web site <www. sglycabettus.gr>. This luxury hotel sits at the foot of Mount Lycabettus and enjoys panoramic views across the city. Ask for a room facing south for this view out of your window. A major renovation program in the late 1990s has updated reception areas to produce a modern yet refined feel. Rooms have A/C, TV, phone, mini-bar. Facilities include two restaurants, room service, roof pool in summer, parking. 158 rooms. Major credit cards.

Athenian Inn \$\$ Odós Haritos; Tel: (01) 723 8097; fax (01) 724 2268. Set on a quiet street in the middle of the Kolonaki area yet an easy stroll to the central attractions, this small hotel puts you at the heart of great shopping and numerous restaurants. Most rooms have a balcony though only the upper floors have any real view — out towards Lycabettus. Rooms have A/C, TV, phone, mini-bar. Facilities include restaurant, bar. 28 rooms. Major credit cards.

MEGARON

Andromeda Hotel and Apartments $$$$$ Odós Timoleontos Vassou 22, GR-115 21 Athens; Tel. (01) 643 7302; fax (01) 646 6361. Set on a quiet side street near the US Embassy, Andromeda is a classic small boutique hotel and one of the best places in Athens to enjoy a luxurious personal service. Each room is individually designed and all feature works by renowned artists and designers. The White Elephant restaurant is part of the same complex. Rooms have A/C, TV, mini-bar, phone, dataport. Facilities include restaurant, bar. 21 standard rooms, 12 apartments Major credit cards.

Divani Caravel $$$$$ Avenue Vassileos Alexandrou 2, 116 10 Athens; Tel. (01) 725 3725; fax (01) 725 3770; web site <www.divani.gr>. Situated close to the National Gallery and Evangelismos Metro station, the Divani Caravel is a large, luxury hotel with numerous facilities for the traveler. Rooms have A/C, satellite TV, phone, mini-bar, safe, hairdryer, voice mail facilities, and data port. Facilities include restaurant, bar, 24-hour room service, year-round swimming pool with views of the city, fitness room, shopping, hairdresser, parking. 471 rooms. Major credit cards.

Alexandros Hotel $$$ Odós Timoleontos Vassou 8, GR-115 21 Athens; Tel. (01) 643 0464; fax (01) 644 1084. Located in a quiet side street near the US Embassy, the Alexandros offers comfortable accommodations with modern furnishings though the exterior is a little dour. Favored by businessmen for its service, it is a good medium-priced option for independent travelers who don't need the help of concierge services. Rooms have A/C, TV, phone, mini-bar. Facilities include parking. Open year-round. 96 rooms. Major credit cards.

PLAKA

Adrian Hotel $$ Odós Adrianou 74, 105 56 Athens; Tel. (01) 322 1553; fax (01) 325 0461. This small, simple hotel is situated in the heart of Plaka and you can stroll to all the major sites. It can be a little noisy in the evenings with a square full of bars and cafés situated outside the entrance — but this is the atmosphere of the district. Rooms at the front of the hotel have balconies with street and square views. Rooms have A/C, TV, phone, mini-bar, safe. Facilities include roof garden with view of the Acropolis. Open year-round. 22 rooms. Major credit cards.

OMONIA

Omonia Grand Hotel $$$ Odós Pireos 2, 105 52 Athens; Tel. (01) 523 5230; fax (01) 523 1361. A brand new hotel on Omonia Square with modern design and décor to bring a touch of glamour to the square. Small lobby but the rooms are well-furnished and those on the upper floors have views of Lycabettus. Rooms have A/C, soundproofing, TV, phone, dataport, mini-bar, safe. Facilities include restaurant, bar. Open year-round. 112 Rooms. Major credit cards.

Hotel Jason $$ Odós Nikiforou 3, 104 37 Athens; Tel. (01) 523 3030; fax (01) 523 4786. In a small side street near Omonia Square, this hotel doesn't win any awards for design but offers reasonable accommodations close to shopping and Metro connections to other areas of the city. Rooms have

A/C, TV, phone. Facilities include breakfast room. Open year-round. 82 rooms. Major credit cards.

SYNGROU

Metropolitan Hotel $$$$$ Avenue Syngrou 385, 175 64 Athens; Tel. (01) 9471000; fax (01) 9471010; web site <www.chandris.gr>. Situated 10 minutes south of the Acropolis on Syngrou arterial route, the Metropolitan makes a good base for those who want to be a little out of the hubbub. Rooms have A/C, TV, phone, hairdryer, mini-bar, safe. Facilities include shuttle bus to and from Syntagma Square, two restaurants, three bars, roof pool in summer, fitness room. 24-hour room service. 361 rooms. Major credit cards.

Acropolis Select $$–$$$ Odós Farlirou 37–39, Athens; Tel. (01) 921 1611; fax (01) 921 6938. Recently renovated, this pension-style hotel offers accommodations above its class with comfortable rooms and modern furnishings. Located one block west of Syngrou in the shadow of Philopappas Hill, it's only a stroll from the downtown area. Rooms have A/C, TC, phone, mini-bar. Facilities include parking. 72 rooms. Major credit cards.

SYNTAGMA SQUARE

Grande Bretagne $$$$$ Odós Vassileos Georgiou Aí; Tel: (01) 333 0000; fax (01) 322 8034; web site <www. sheraton.com>. Perhaps the most famous hotel in Athens, the Grande Bretagne is a Neo-Classical building set directly on Syntagma Square. Antique furniture and period detail abounds though in some places the finishings are showing their age. For history, atmosphere, and location it's still difficult to beat. Rooms have A/C, TV, phone, mini-bar, nonsmoking rooms. Facilities include two restaurants, bar, no smoking area, parking. Open year-round. 261 rooms. Major credit cards.

Olympic Palace $$–$$$ Odós Philellinon 16; Tel: (01) 323 7611; fax (01) 322 5583. A modern hotel recently refurbished and centrally located, the Olympic Palace attracts businessmen in addition to tourists. Rooms on the upper floor have views of the Acropolis. Rooms have A/C, TV, phone, mini-bar. Facilities include restaurant, 24-hour room service, parking. Open year-round. 90 rooms. Major credit cards.

Electra Hotel $$$ Odós Ermou 5, 105 56 Athens; Tel. (01) 322 3223; fax (01) 322 0310; e-mail <electrahotels@ ath.forthnet.gr>. Centrally located just off Syntagma Square the Electra offers a good location though a rather unexciting product. Perfect for those who want to spend most of their time exploring the city and need few frills. Rooms have A/C, TV, phone, mini-bar. Facilities include bar, restaurant. Open year-round. 110 rooms. Major credit cards.

Amalia Hotel $$$ Leoforos Amalias 10, 105 57 Athens; Tel. (01) 323 7301; fax (01) 323 8792. Comfortable, modern hotel situated directly across from the National Gardens — so close to Plaka, the archaeological sites, and the major museums. It is a relatively quiet hotel for such a central location. Rooms at the front have views of Lycabettus and the Parliament building. Rooms have A/C, TV, phone. Facilities include restaurant, bar, parking. Open year-round. 90 rooms. Major credit cards.

EXCURSION LOCATIONS

Candia House $$$$–$$$$$ 211 00 Kandia, Ireon, Nafplio; Tel. (0752) 94060; fax (0752) 94480; web site

<www.candiahouse.gr>. Candia House is a small personal luxury hotel owned by a delightful Athenian lady, an ex-publisher, who wanted to create a peaceful haven for her guests. Located 20 km (12 miles) from Nafplio on a sandy beach, it is ideally placed for touring the Argolid area. Each individually designed and furnished suite has living room, A/C, TV, phone, kitchen, balcony. Facilities include pool, bar, restaurant serving wholefoods, gym, sauna. Open May–Oct. 10 suites. Major credit cards.

Hotel Rex $$ Odós Bouboulinas 21, 211 00 Nafplio; Tel. (0752) 26907; fax (0752) 28106. Located in Nafplio and just outside the old town, the Rex has been recently refurbished with elegant foyers belying its class. Rooms are more simply furnished but are clean and spacious. A good base for exploring town and the surrounding area. Rooms have TV, phone, mini-bar, balcony. Facilities include restaurant, bar. Open year-round. 42 rooms. Major credit cards.

Hotel Seven Brothers $ Poros Town; Tel. (0298) 23412; fax (0298) 23413. Situated at the corner of a little square just off the seafront, the Seven Brothers puts you at the heart of pretty Poros Town. The rooms are simply furnished but have balconies. Rooms have A/C, TV, mini-bar. A comfortable budget option. Open April–Oct (for winter openings call ahead and speak to the owner). 19 rooms. Major credit cards.

Hotel Amalia $$$–$$$$ Delphi; Tel. (0265) 82101; fax (0265) 82290. Historic country hotel set in 3.5 hectares (8.5 acres) of gardens and wonderful views over the Bay of Itea. This is the place to come for a luxury overnight stop—to be able to visit Delphi late or early in the day, before the tour buses arrive. Rooms have A/C, TV, phone. Facilities include restaurant, bar, pool. Open year-round. 180 rooms. Major credit cards.

Olympic Hotel $ Odós Droseros, Delphi; Tel. (0265) 82780; fax (0265) 82780. Small new hotel at the far end of Delphi village with far-reaching views across the Itea valley to the sea from rooms at the back; these have small balconies. Good option for budget travelers—rooms are well furnished if a little small. You can stroll to a number of village tavernas. Friendly owners. Rooms have A/C, TV. Facilities include breakfast room. Open April–Nov. 20 rooms. Cash only.

Eginitiko Aronitiko $ Aegina; Tel. (0298) 24968; fax (0298) 26716. An 18th century mansion expanded during the 19th century and now converted into a small pension hotel with a personal touch. Wonderful period furniture through-out, and ornate painted ceilings in the communal rooms. Two patios and a courtyard. Rooms have A/C and phone. Open year-round. 12 rooms. Cash only.

Economou Mansion $ On the harborfront, Hydra; Tel. (0298) 734001; fax (0298) 74074. Neo-Classical mansion on the water's edge and just a short walk from the main harbor and the town, beautifully renovated with period furniture in all rooms. A very relaxing place to stay. Open year-round. 4 rooms. Cash only.

Nissia $$$ Coast Road, Spetses Town, Spetses; Tel. (0298) 75000; fax (0298) 75012. Set 500 m (1,600 ft) from the harbor with magnificent views of the town, the Nissia is designed in traditional style with suites, studios, and apart-ments—each individually furnished—that can accommo-date couples and families. Each unit has A/C, TV, kitchen. Facilities include pool, restaurant, bar, room service. Buffet breakfast included in the price. 29 units. Major credit cards.

Recommended Restaurants

Athens offers an astounding range of culinary opportunities and is home to a number of outstanding restaurants—Greeks themselves enjoy eating out which keeps pressure on the industry to maintain and improve on its standards. Follow the local people for the best cuisine—which may not be in the prettiest settings —and you will not be disappointed. Many Athens restaurants close during the summer months. Some of the most renowned move to the coast to a secondary location as Athenians escape the worst of the city heat. Many also close on Sundays.

Not all restaurants accept credit cards, so always ask if this is your preferred method of payment. Smoking is a popular habit in Greece and few restaurants have a no-smoking section—eating in the open air (in itself a pleasure) is often the only way to escape the smoke.

Few restaurants accept reservations but if you plan to eat at one of the finer establishment this would be wise on weekends.

The following recommendations include restaurants and tavernas serving Greek cuisine, and a range of established and well-regarded restaurants serving international cuisine. Most lie within the downtown area close to public transport routes or a short taxi ride from central hotels. To make a telephone enquiry or booking, the numbers below have the regional code included. Always preface the number with the international code 00 30 and drop the first 0 from the district code if you are calling from outside Greece.

Prices indicated are for dinner per person without wine.

> **$** under 5,000drs.
> **$$** 5,000–7,000drs.
> **$$$** 7,000–9,000drs.
> **$$$$** 9,000–12,000drs.
> **$$$$$** over 12,000drs.

ACROPOLIS (MAKRIYANNI)

Edodi $$$$$ Odós Veikou 80; Tel. (01) 921 3013. One of the best "modern" restaurants in the city and run by two brothers of high renown. The fusion international menu changes regularly but will always be beautifully presented. This is the place to come for an event rather than a simple meal. Reservations recommended. Open Mon–Sat 6pm–midnight (closed August). Major credit cards.

Dionysus $$–$$$ Odós Rovertou Gali 43; Tel: (01) 923 3182. Stunning views of the Acropolis makes Dionysus a must for all visitors to Athens. It sits on the north side very near the Sound and Light Show. Totally refurbished and expanded in the late 1990s, it now accepts tour groups as well as individual tables. Classic Greek and international dishes, all well-prepared. Open daily 11am–3pm, 6pm–11pm. Major credit cards.

Strofi $$ Odós Rovertou Galli 25; Tel. (01) 921 4130. An excellent range of Greek cuisine with salads, grilled and stewed dishes and seafood options. The view of the Acropolis is outstanding and makes Strofi one of the bargain eateries in town — in most other cities in the world you'd pay a premium for this location! Open Mon–Sat 8pm–2am. Major credit cards.

KOLONAKI

Boschetto $$$$$ Alsos Evangelisomos; Tel: (01) 721 0893. One of the smartest restaurants in the downtown area (near the Byzantine Museum), Boschetto offers summer dining among the fragrant pines or a beautiful interior dining area for more chilly winter weather. Grand dining with Mediterranean dishes and a varied seafood selection. Good wine list. Reservations are recommended, as this restaurant is a favorite. Open all year, Mon–Sat 6pm–11pm. Major credit cards.

Kallimarmaron $$ Odós Eufroniou 13; Tel. (01) 701 9727. Traditional dishes served in a homey environment makes this restaurant a good place to begin your exploration of Greek cuisine. The roasted lamb and stewed dishes are very tasty, but don't limit yourself to these. There are a lot of other succulent choices. The restaurant is close to the Hilton and Divani Caravel Hotels. Open Tues–Sat 11am–2:30pm, 6pm–11pm (closed in August). Major credit cards.

Kiku $$$$–$$$$$ Odós Dimokritou 12; Tel. (01) 364 7033. One of the best places to eat Japanese cuisine in Athens, this restaurant in the Kolonaki area caters to a faithful clientele and Japanese tourists who want a taste of home. A full range of dishes on the menu—the sushi is excellent. Open Mon–Sat 6pm–11pm (closed August). Major credit cards.

Jackson Hall $$ Odós Milioni 4; Tel: (01) 361 6098. A combination of 1960s music and large screen TVs recreates the "sports bar" feel of the United States. Menu includes burgers, steaks, and salads washed down with cold beer or hot American coffee. Set in one of the busiest pedestrian streets in the city. Open daily all year 11am–11pm. Major credit cards.

L'Abreuvoir $$$–$$$$ Odós Xenocratous 51; Tel. (01) 722 9106. Classic French cuisine in this longstanding restaurant now in the second generation of ownership. Enjoy the smart interior dining room or eat out under the trees in summer. Everything from filet mignon to crepes. Good wine list. Open daily all year 11am–2pm, 6pm–11pm. Major credit cards.

Kafenio $$ Odós Loukianou 26; Tel. (01) 722 9056. Good "home cooking"-style taverna, which has a faithful Athenian following. The roasted piglet is some of the best in the capital but there is a menu of fresh seasonal dishes for you to try. Air-conditioned dining room or outside dining in the summer. Open Mon–Sat 11am–2:30pm, 7pm–11pm (closed in August). Cash only.

MEGARON

White Elephant $$$$$ Odós Timoleontos Vassou 22; Tel: (01) 643 7302. Situated a stroll away from the US embassy, the White Elephant is one of the trendiest restaurants in the city, and is featured regularly in top 10 lists. Its Polynesian cuisine is prepared with finesse, and with the freshest ingredients. The flavors are full and the fusion of ingredients makes for an interesting menu. Open Mon–Sat 11am–4pm, 7pm–11pm. Major credit cards.

MONASTIRAKI/PSIRI

Interni $$$$$ Odós Ermou 152; Tel. (01) 346 8900. One of the most fashionable eateries in Athens, with minimalist architectural design and exceptional cuisine; concentrating on Italian dishes with a selection of classical French entrées. A wonderful central location where you'll be joined by the smart "set." Open Oct–April (summers on Mykonos island) Mon–Sat 7pm–late. Major credit cards.

Evipros $ Odós Navarhou Apostoli 3, Psiri; Tel. (01) 323 1351. Very good taverna in the "non-touristy" district of central Athens. Extremely good pies and slow-cooked meat dishes—rabbit is a specialty when in season. Modern décor. Open daily 11am–3pm, 6pm–midnight (closed August). Major credit cards.

Savvas \$ Odós Mitropoleos 86; Tel. (01) 321 3201. One of the best cheap eateries in the city and a perfect place to stop for souvlaki after strolling around the flea market. Take-out or eat at the few tables nearby. Open daily 8am–3am. Cash only.

OMONIA

Diporto \$\$ Corner Odós Theatro and Sofokleous; No phone. Located at the edge of the central market, Diporto attracts a range of clientele from stallholders to businesspeople. Salads, grilled fish, and one-pot stewed dishes are on the menu—all extremely well cooked. Good retsina. Open daily 6am–6pm. Cash only.

Ideal \$\$ Odós Panepistimiou 46; Tel. (01) 330 3000. One of the most established restaurants in the city, Ideal offers excellent, taverna-style food. The stewed dishes are excellent as is the moussaka. This makes an excellent introduction to the Greek cuisine and will help you to spot imitation home cooking as you travel around the city. Open Mon–Sat 11am–3pm, 6pm–11pm. Major credit cards.

Athinaikon \$ Odós Themistokleous 2; Tel. (01) 383 8485. One of the best places in central Athens to have *meze* dishes —whatever the time of day. Very busy at lunchtimes with business people, and you can watch the world go by as you eat. Open Mon–Sat 11:30am–1am (closed in August). Cash only.

PLAKA

Eden $$ Odós Lissiou 12; Tel. (01) 324 8858. One of the few vegetarian restaurants in the downtown area, Eden is housed in a pretty Neo-Classical mansion. The menu includes vegetarian versions of Greek dishes and a range of fresh salads. Open daily 11am–midnight. Major credit cards.

Stou Xynou $$ Odós Angelou Geronda 4; Tel. (01) 322 0165. An old-style taverna with exceptionally tasty food and refreshing retsina, live music, and a garden setting. A great place to escape to real Greece from the sometimes over-touristy streets of Plaka. Open Mon–Fri 7pm–1am (closed in July). Major credit cards.

To Xavi $–$$ Odós Adrianou 138; Tel. (01) 322 8966. Most visitors want to sit and eat on one of Plaka's streets and soak in the summer atmosphere. This taverna sits in the heart of the district and has tables on the street and beside large windows. The food, though not spectacular, is fine—with a good range on the menu. Live music most evenings. Open daily 11am–1am. Major credit cards.

Kostas $ Odós Adrianou 116; No phone. Simply a hole in the wall souvlaki stall with no tables or chairs, but Kostas is famed throughout Athens for his succulent grilled meat and gyros. You'll always see a line leading to the little counter window. The perfect snack while strolling along Plaka's pretty streets. Open Mon–Sat 10am–11pm. Cash only.

Bakaliarakia (tou Damigou) $ Odós Kydathineon 41; Tel: (01) 322 5084. A traditional "koutouki" or under-ground taverna, which has been earning accolades for generations, this is a place to come and find genuine atmosphere and excellent Greek food. Famed for its codfish and pan-fried potatoes. Open Mon–Sat 6pm–11pm (closed in August). Cash only.

Platanos $ Odós Diogenous 4; Tel: (01) 322 0666. Situated in a small square near the Musical Instrument Museum, this small taverna offers a limited menu of well-cooked Greek dishes including oven-stewed lamb and pork of melting tenderness. In summer sit out under the large plane tree. Open daily 11am–3pm, 6pm–11pm (closed in August). Cash only.

SYNGROU AVE

Mezzo-Mezzo $$$$$ Ave Sygrou 58; Tel: (01) 924 2444. Set in a refurbished 19th century building, Mezzo-Mezzo is an open plan restaurant decorated with Greek art by the most renowned modern artists and frequented by the Athens glitterati. The menu is modern with a fusion of French, Italian, and Far Eastern influences. In summer the restaurant moves to a location in Voula by the coast. Open at the Athens location September–May. Open Mon–Sat 6pm–11pm. Major credit cards.

EXCURSION LOCATIONS

Agora $–$$ At the fish market, Aegina Town; Tel. (0298) 27308. Found in the heart of town and near a small park, the Agora was opened 40 years ago. Excellent fish dishes comprising whatever the catch brings in so you can be sure that it's always fresh. Open year-round daily 11am–11pm. Cash only.

Dourabeis $$$ Akti Protopsalti 27, Piraeus; Tel. (01) 412 2092. Renowned throughout the region for over 60 years, Dourebeis has a loyal local following. They serve an excellent range of seafood with extremely good grilled whole fish or fillets, and tasty shellfish or octopus. These are accompanied by crisp fresh salads. Open year-round daily 6pm–11pm. Cash only.

Kanaris (Karamanlis) $ Odós Bouboulinas 1, Nafplio; Tel. (0572) 27668. Set on a pretty, cobbled traffic-free street, Kanaris is a very good taverna specializing in oven-cooked dishes made with seasonal ingredients. Favorite restaurant of Greek Prime Minister Konstantinos Karamanlis during his lifetime. Open year-round daily 11am–11pm. Cash only.

Kondylenia $$–$$$ Kaminia, Hydra; Tel. (0298) 53520. With a fantastic view over the sea from the veranda, the food at this taverna needs to be good. You won't be disappointed. The menu features traditional meat and seafood dishes, with seasonal local ingredients. Open from Lent–October daily 11am–11pm. Major credit cards.

Taverna Vakchos $–$$ Odós Apollonon 32, Delphi; Tel. (0265) 82448. This family-run restaurant serves excellent seasonal Greek cuisine—including wild boar in winter. The slow-cooked dishes are extremely tasty, salads crisp, and the village wine fresh and cool. A really good example of what Greek tavernas are all about. You can also get breakfast here. Open year-round Mon–Sat 8am–11pm. Major credit cards.

Vyzantino $ Old Harbour, Spetses Town; Tel. (0298) 72870. An old stone building with pretty terrace overlooking the harbor, Vyzantino is one of the best ouzeries on Spetses. Excellent mezedes dishes to accompany your drinks or make up a main meal. Open Greek Easter–September daily 11am–11pm. Cash only.

INDEX